THIS ENGLAND
ANNUAL 2021

Celebrate the best of England

Events • People • Places • Views

Welcome

This is our first book-style *This England* Annual and it's like an annual of old – hard covers to keep it ship-shape and perfect for dipping into. We have quizzes to challenge you, poetry and plenty of articles to entertain.

After 2020 being the year of lockdown, we hope that 2021 will be the year when everything opens up again. Our seasonal guides take you around the country to discover our customs from the big events of the year to the far more obscure – whether it's snail racing in Congham or the Framlingham sausage festival.

There's plenty more besides, including beautiful towns to explore and stunning photography. Discover our favourite pubs, our favourite birds and where to see Christmas decorations at their best. We hope you enjoy our annual!

Angela

Angela Linforth, Editor

CONTENTS

WINTER TO SPRING

SPRING TO SUMMER

10

42

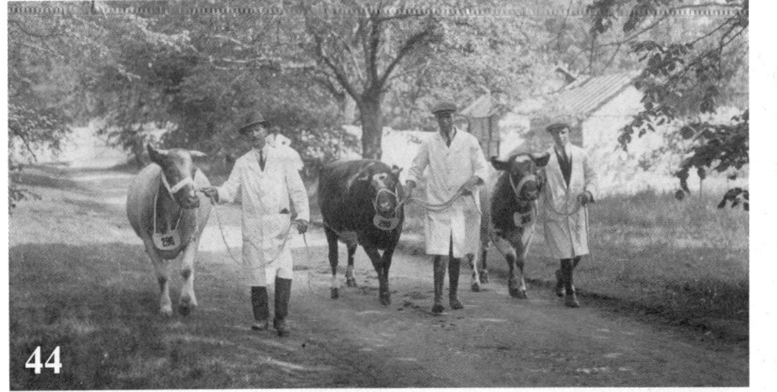

44

34

100

SUMMER TO AUTUMN

AUTUMN TO WINTER

68

90

Front cover: Botallack, Cornwall. Back cover: Bewl Water, Kent. Cover images by David Sellman.

Winter Into Spring

by Richard Lackman

From March back through November
landscapes draped in black and white
As knife-like shadows in the forests
pierced the dimming light
And even mighty rivers disappeared
under the strain
Of crushing floes of ice after a night
of freezing rain

For now the only sounds that crackle
out through winter's hush
Are frozen pods of snow which to the
ground from treetops rush
Exploding on the forest floor as from
a fearsome horde
Of Norsemen fighting wildly for their
own wintry warlord

And so it is that through the coldest
season of the year
We sequester deep within the halls
that we hold dear
Waiting for the sunrise and the
promise it will bring
That the stranglehold of winter will be
broken by the spring

Then finally it happens; ice floes melt
and streams cascade
Flowers bloom and fruit trees blossom
while the pall of winter fades
Black and white are all forgotten as a
rainbow now appears
And the cycle reinvigorates the
passing of the years

Watendlath Beck in the Lake District

Images: Getty. Poem first published by the Society of Classical Poetry

WINTER TO SPRING

Events of the season, a Goon Show anniversary, Britain's best pubs and a chance to test yourself with our great geography quiz >

WINTER TO SPRING

From slapstick in Bristol to a wife-carrying competition in Dorking, Katherine Sorrell recommends the best events this spring

JANUARY 2021

NEW YEAR'S DAY PARADE

The capital kicks off the New Year in style with a parade that's billed as "the world's greatest street spectacular", and features thousands of performers from all around the world, including cheer squads and marching bands, floats and inflatables, clowns, dancers and groups from West End shows. It starts at noon at Piccadilly Circus and winds its way via Pall Mall and Trafalgar Square to a grand finish in Parliament Square. Arrive early to get a good spot!
London; lnydp.com

The New Year's Day Parade in London attracts vistors from afar

BURNS NIGHT

It's a Scottish tradition that's widely celebrated in England, too – commemorating the birthday (on 25 January) and legacy of great and prolific poet Robert Burns. There will be poetry, bagpipes, plenty of whisky and, of course, haggis – a great excuse for a party!
One of the best is at London's Ceilidh Club, which hosts three hours of dancing to a live band and caller. At halftime, the haggis is piped in and Burns's poem, *Address to a Haggis*, is recited. The bar serves haggis, neeps (turnips) and tatties (potatoes) buffet-style, and the finale of the evening is a rendition of Burns's most famous poem, *Auld Lang Syne*.
London; ceilidhclub.com

Haggis with neeps and tatties

PLOUGH SUNDAY AND MONDAY

Plough Monday, the first Monday after Twelfth Night, was traditionally the start of the English agricultural year, with farm workers returning to the fields. In parts of the country it was common for men with soot-blackened faces (to avoid recognition by future employers) to drag a plough through their villages, collecting money while singing, dancing and performing plays. The local church blessed the plough, on the same day or on Plough Sunday. Records of such celebrations go back to the 15th century and, though less common today, still exist in some parts of the country, including Durham. Expect Morris dancing, mummers, parades, fancy dress and festive cheer.
durhamcathedral.co.uk/news/plough-Sunday

Marking Plow Monday in the 1700s

THE WASSAIL

From the Anglo-Saxon phrase "waes hael", which means good health, wassailing is a traditional custom intended to bring luck. Hundreds of local wassailing events take place each year around Christmas and early in the New Year, usually in the form of either groups that visit local properties to sing folk songs and bring good cheer, or an orchard wassail in which evil spirits are banished and the trees blessed to encourage the crop.

In Sussex and Surrey this is known as "howling" – and shouting, banging tin trays and generally making a racket are encouraged as part of the ceremony, as well as firing shotguns into the trees to wake them up and placing pieces of toast in the branches to attract good spirits (the original meaning of the phrase "to toast"). There may well be a procession, songs and dancing, and a wassail drink, usually a local ale or cider blended with honey and spices. Some National Trust properties hold wassailing events. You can also try:

Morris dancing at a wassail

- The Cider Works in Crediton, Devon, where the entertainment includes a wassail play, a fire dance and a ceremony where the local Green Man is the MC. **sandfordorchards.co.uk**
- Pilgrim Morris perform a wassail around the pubs of Guildford on Twelfth Night each year, singing traditional carols, performing the Guildford Mummers Play and generously passing round the wassail bowl. **pilgrimmorrismen.org.uk**
- Carhampton Community Orchard, where there is a traditional combination of songs, refreshments and ceremony. **facebook.com/events/149205989053393**

The Green Man often blesses the orchard

- Bodmin Wassail, a custom first recorded in 1624, in which a group of men dressed in top hat and tails visits care homes, pubs, businesses and people's homes, singing traditional songs and collecting for charity. **bodminwassail.uk**
- Bolney apple howling, led by the Chanctonbury Ring Morris Men at a local fruit farm, includes a torchlit procession and "general hullabaloo". **crmm.org.uk**

KATHERINE JENKINS LIVE

The classical crossover star begins her 2021 tour on 24 January at the O2 Guildhall in Southampton, singing songs from her new, movie-inspired album, *Cinema Paradiso*. **Southampton, Hampshire; katherinejenkins.co.uk**

Katherine Jenkins sings

SNOWDROPS TO SEE

A good swathe of snowdrops (*Galanthus*) is one of the first cheery signs of spring. There are plenty of places to see them and some of our favourites include the Wallington Estate, near Morpeth, Nortumberland. Attingham Park near Shrewsbury, Shropshire, has a stunning carpet of snowdrops. Newark Park, a Grade-I-listed Tudor country house, near Wotton-under-Edge, Gloucestershire has a fine display, as does Kingston Lacey, with 50,000 bulbs to see, near Wimborne in Dorset.

STRAW BEAR FESTIVAL

A man wrapped in a coat of straw makes quite a sight in the town of Whittlesea. It's the revival of an ancient tradition that's linked to Plough Monday (see left-hand page), though no-one quite knows where it originated. These days there's a three-day festival, with the finale on the Saturday involving more than 250 dancers, musicians and performers performing traditional Molly, Morris, Clog and Sword as the "bear" is led along the street.

It all ends with a ceremonial burning of the costume on Sunday.

Whittlesea, Cambridgeshire; strawbear.org.uk

Three straw bears are led through the streets during the annual Whittlesea Straw Bear Festival parade

>

SLAPSTICK FESTIVAL

If you enjoy the humour of the stars of the silent screen – Charlie Chaplin, Buster Keaton, Harold Lloyd and more – you'll love Bristol's annual celebration of slapstick. The festival, which started in 2005, brings together guest comedians, experts and film historians in a passionate and hilarious celebration of classic silent and physical comedy. The aim of the festival is to introduce a wider audience to the charms of silent film.
Bristol; slapstick.org.uk

Charlie Chaplin, king of slapstick, during the shooting of the film Modern Times, *1936*

HAXEY HOOD

The Haxey Hood is one of the oldest local traditions in England, probably dating back to the 14th century. On 6 January each year, the town near Doncaster takes part in a mass game that's a kind of huge rugby scrum or "sway" with very few rules, the aim being to manoeuvre the "hood" (a two-foot length of strong leather) towards one of the pubs or guest-houses in the parish. With around 200 people in the slow-moving sway, and a thousand or so watching, the whole thing is presided over by a Lord, Fool and referees known as Boggins, who in the week preceding tour local pubs wearing their festival costumes and singing traditional folk songs.
Haxey, North Lincolnshire; wheewall.com/hood

Right: Chief Boggin Ian Dawes at the start of a Haxey Hood

Many villagers battle for the Haxey Hood in this traditional game at Haxey Village in Doncaster

HOLLY HOLY DAY

On 25 January, 1644, the siege of Nantwich was lifted by Parliamentary forces and, to commemorate the battle, the town holds an annual day of celebration – called Holly Holy Day, because the locals wore sprigs of holly in their hats. As well as a parade and battle re-enactment by several hundred troops from the Sealed Knot society, there's live music, refreshments, Morris dancing and a wreath-laying ceremony.
Nantwich, Cheshire; battleofnantwich.org

The battle re-enactment

LONDON ART FAIR

Returning on 20-24 January, London Art Fair is an unmissable opening to the international art calendar. See works from more than 100 galleries from around the world presenting the great names of 20th-century modern British art, plus exceptional contemporary work. There are plenty of talks and the fair is aimed at both the seasoned and aspiring collector.
Islington, N1; londonartfair.co.uk

The London Art Fair at the Design Centre, Islington

GRIMALDI SERVICE

The clowns get together

Joseph Grimaldi is known as the king of clowns, and scores of professional clowns of all descriptions, in full costume, pack the pews for this popular annual service (on the first Sunday in February) that includes hymns, readings, songs and even performances.
All Saints Church, Haggerston, London; clownsinternational.com

ORCHIDS

For a blast of colour early in the year, the annual orchid festival at Kew can't be beaten. The impressive Princess of Wales conservatory is given over to this beautiful flower, sourced mainly from one country. Previous displays have paid homage to Indonesia, Brazil, Thailand and India. The orchid displays are usually breathtaking and complemented with music and often street food from the country. There are also a series of talks from Kew's orchid experts and evening viewings in Kew's After Hours programme.
Kew Gardens, Richmond; Kew.org

Extravagant costumes in Chinatown, London

CHINESE NEW YEAR

London's Chinese New Year celebrations are the biggest outside Asia, and involve hundreds of thousands of people descending on Chinatown in the West End for parades, performances and plenty of food. Major events for the year of the Ox, which begins on 12 February, will also take place in other cities, including Manchester, Liverpool, Birmingham, Southampton and elsewhere around the country.

HURLING THE SILVER BALL

The St Ives Feast Day, on the first Monday after 3 February, starts with a civic procession for the blessing at St Ia's Well near Porthmeor Beach, followed by one of Cornwall's most ancient traditions: the "hurling" of a silver ball. In this boisterous game, participants attempt to win the cricket-ball-sized ball from each other around the town (and sometimes in the sea). Whoever returns the ball to the mayor on the steps of St Ives Guildhall on the stroke of midday receives a silver coin. In the afternoon, pennies are proffered from the balcony by town councillors to waiting children on the Guildhall forecourt.
St Ives, Cornwall; stives-cornwall.co.uk/events/st-ives-feast-day

A competitor in the sea during the silver ball hurling, 1956

DÜRER'S JOURNEYS

The first major UK exhibition of Albrecht Dürer in nearly 20 years features paintings, drawings, prints and letters following the German Renaissance artist's travels across Europe, bringing to life the artist himself and the people and places he visited.
From 13 February-16 May. Sainsbury Wing, The National Gallery, London; nationalgallery.org.uk

THE LONDON CLASSIC CAR SHOW

For anyone who appreciates the fine lines of a classic car, there's nowhere better to be than London's Olympia from 18-21 February, where you can see (and even buy) some of the world's most desirable vehicles and celebrate iconic marques from decades past.
Olympia, London; thelondonclassiccarshow.co.uk

SLAITHWAITE MOONRAKING FESTIVAL

The story goes that a band of smugglers used to hide their illegal bounty, brought in by narrowboat, under the village's canal bridge. On the night of a full

Members of the cathedral choir in the candlelit procession at Ripon Cathedral

CANDLEMAS

To commemorate the presentation of Christ at the Temple, more than 7,000 candles are lit in Ripon Cathedral, in alcoves and in intricate designs on the floor. Hundreds of people attend the spectacular service, usually held on the 2nd of the month.
Ripon Cathedral, Ripon, North Yorkshire; riponcathedral.org.uk

moon, they took their rakes and went to fish out one of the barrels of rum, but were caught in the act by the militia. To avoid arrest, they claimed to be out "moonraking", the reflection of the full moon being clearly seen in the water.

In this festival, a week of willow lantern-making, music workshops and storytelling culminates in a finale where a giant "moon" is floated along the canal on a raft before being paraded through the town as part of a carnival of samba drums, jazz bands and locals all carrying their own candlelit lanterns. The festival takes place every two years, on the odd year.
Slaithwaite, West Yorkshire; slaithwaitemoonraking.org.uk

Forced rhubarb is celebrated in Wakefield

RHUBARB FESTIVAL

The district of Wakefield has a long tradition of rhubarb-growing and in this, usually the first major food festival of the calendar year, you'll find speciality market stalls, food demonstrations, family fun, arts and crafts stalls, exhibitions, comedy, live music and special events. Plus, of course, there are sticks and sticks of early rhubarb, plus a Rhu-Bar to enjoy.
Wakefield, Yorkshire; experiencewakefield.co.uk

IMAGINE CHILDREN'S FESTIVAL

Liven up a half-term week with 12 days of some of the best international performance, music, literature, comedy, creativity, parties, participation and free fun for children aged 0-11 and their grown-ups. This is the largest festival of its kind in the UK, Imagine Children's Festival is dedicated to families experiencing and enjoying all kinds of art and culture together.
Southbank Centre, London; southbankcentre.co.uk

50 YEARS AGO

DECIMAL DAY

It was 50 years ago this month that Britain abandoned shillings, threepenny bits, half-crowns and guineas, in favour of a decimalised currency, minting 3.4 billion coins for the changeover. It was a gargantuan logistical effort that took five years of preparation – but in the end went remarkably smoothly (so much so that the European Commission later studied it in its preparation for launching the euro). The British Museum's exhibition commemorates D-Day with a social record amassed from recollections sent in by members of the public, as well as objects from its collection, including cash registers, ready reckoners and government posters showing conversion rates.
British Museum, London; britishmuseum.org

Lord Fiske in Woolworths on Decimal Day

SIX NATIONS RUGBY

England's home matches for the Six Nations Championship take place at London's Twickenham Stadium, with the first – the Calcutta Cup match against Scotland – taking place on the opening day, Saturday 6 February.
The tournament runs until 20 March; sixnationsrugby.com

JORVIK VIKING FESTIVAL

Jolablot was a raucous Viking celebration of the arrival of spring and the end of winter hardships. Taking place at the same time of year (or in modern times half-term) this annual family-friendly festival, the largest of its kind in Europe, celebrates York's heritage of almost a century of Viking rule.

Listen to Norse sagas and stories, pick up a sword, meet "real" Vikings and learn about their crafts, visit a reconstructed village and watch spectacular battle re-enactments.

York; jorvikvikingfestival.co.uk

Viking re-enactors have a rest as they wait to march through York

KESWICK FILM FESTIVAL

Cumbria's answer to Sundance, this acclaimed festival offers a programme of the best of world and independent cinema, with everything from blockbusters to thought-provoking documentaries, plus retrospectives and special guests.

Keswick, Cumbria; keswickfilmclub.org

DERBY WINTER BEER FESTIVAL

Dubbed the Real Ale Capital of Britain, Derby hosts this four-day festival in one of its iconic railway buildings, the Roundhouse. This homage to ales, lagers and ciders has bands and tastings, with visitors exploring the city while sampling beers from its microbreweries.

Derby; derby.camra.org.uk/winter-beer-festival

DARK SKIES FESTIVAL

National Parks remain some of the darkest places in Great Britain, and this fortnight-long festival celebrates the South Downs International Dark Skies Reserve designation, and is set to include star parties, talks, observations and other family activities.

South Downs National Park; darkskiesnationalparks.org.uk

Women of Olney in Buckinghamshire racing in 1920

EVENTS ON SHROVE TUESDAY

Shrove Tuesday (this year falling on 16 February) is the day before the start of Lent and, of course, is followed by Ash Wednesday. But did you know that the day before Shrove Tuesday is known as Collop Monday? There are many traditional customs observed around the country at this time, often centred on the ideas of using up eggs by making pancakes, and letting off steam in the form of boisterous games, before the penitential season begins.

These include:

- The pancake race at Olney in Buckinghamshire, which first took place in 1445 and is now world famous. It is open only to female residents of the town, who must wear an apron and headscarf and carry a frying pan and pancake. Look out for other pancake races up and down the country.
- "Mob" football matches at Alnwick Castle, Northumberland; Ashbourne, Derbyshire; Sedgefield, County Durham; and Atherstone, Warwickshire. Expect few rules and unusual interpretations of what constitutes a pitch and goal. In St Columb Major, Cornwall, a hurling match with a silver ball (like the one in St Ives) is contested between the Townsmen and the Countrymen every year.
- An intriguing custom called Lentsherd in Clovelly, Devon, in which local children drag tin cans down the village's steep cobbled street at dusk, making a deafening noise which is said to banish the devil into the sea before the start of Lent.
- Traditional long-rope skipping, which takes place on Foreshore Road, Scarborough each year. Children are given time off school and the beachfront becomes a centre for family fun.

>

MARCH 2021

UK WIFE-CARRYING RACE

On a Sunday in March, sometimes April, this extraordinary event is run over a course of 380 metres, including water hazards (buckets and water pistols). Rules are that males or females carry a "wife", who must be alive, human, at least 18 years old, can be male or female, and does not need to be the carrier's actual wife. There's a minimum weight, and recognised holds include bridal, piggy-back, shoulder-ride, fireman's, Estonian and Dorking, or reverse Estonian. The winner gets a barrel of local ale and £250 towards competing in the Finnish Wife-carrying Championships.

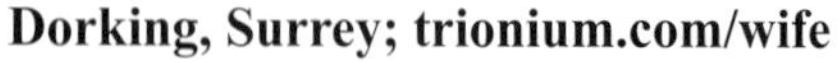

Dorking, Surrey; trionium.com/wife

Competitors carry their wives across an obstacle course in Dorking, Surrey

TICHBORNE DOLE

On Lady Day, or 25 March, each year, local people queue up to claim a gallon of flour each from outside Tichborne House, distributed from a large wooden bin. The charity dole is said to have begun in the late 12th century when Lady Tichborne lay dying and Sir Roger consented to provide a charity from as much land as his wife could walk round holding a lighted torch. She managed to crawl around 23 acres before the torch blew out, and prophesied that the House of Tichborne would fall if the charity were discontinued.
Tichborne, Hampshire.

Warding off a centuries-old curse with flour in 1936 in Tichborne, Hampshire

Pulteney Bridge over the River Avon, Bath

BATH COMEDY FESTIVAL

This springtime extravaganza of laughs usually runs for almost three weeks from late March at venues around the beautiful Georgian city. Featuring household names and newcomers alike, the festival's aim is to bring Bath to life with a vibrant mix of comedy in all its many guises, including stand-up, sketches, film, theatre, writing, art, workshops, music and mystery tours.
bathcomedy.com

WORLD PASTY CHAMPIONSHIPS AND ST PIRAN'S DAY

In a day of music, comedy, food and fun, bakers from around the world compete for the crown of pasty champion. The championships take place on the Saturday before 5 March, which is St Piran's Day, the national day of Cornwall, when a range of festivities are held around the county, from parades and concerts to a mass singing of the Cornish anthem, *Trelawny*.
Eden Project, Cornwall; cornishpastyassociation.co.uk

CRUFTS

Established by Charles Cruft in 1891, this world-famous event attracts 20,000 canine competitors and has become an essential date in any dog lover's calendar. This year it begins on 11 March, with the grand finale, Best in Show, on

the 14th. Look out for Scruffts (for crossbreeds), dog hero competition Friends for Life, and Discover Dogs, where visitors can meet and greet their favourite breeds and find out which ones might be a good match for their lifestyle.
The NEC, Birmingham; crufts.org.uk

THE CHELTENHAM FESTIVAL

One of Britain's favourite horse-racing events, the Cheltenham Festival, is famous for its lively atmosphere, and in particular the roar from the stands as the tape is lifted to start the first race. The iconic festival, which encompasses live music, shopping and world-class food and drink, attracts some of the world's finest horses and jockeys, with royalty often in attendance and celebrities to be seen enjoying champagne and a flutter. It culminates in Gold Cup Day and the prestigious steeplechase, which has given rise to legendary winners including Arkle, Best Mate and the much-loved Desert Orchid.
Cheltenham, Gloucestershire; thejockeyclub.co.uk

A fiery sunset on the shore of Derwentwater, Keswick

WORDS BY THE WATER, KESWICK, CUMBRIA

The leading literature festival in the north-west shares the pleasure of books, words and ideas over 10 days of debate and discussion. Previous years have seen talks by Ben Okri, Melvyn Bragg, Simon Heffer and Jenny Eclair.
Keswick, Cumbria; theatrebythelake.com

ORANGES AND LEMONS CHURCH SERVICE

"Oranges and lemons, say the bells of St Clement's", and the bells of St Clement Danes Church, a Grade-I-listed, 17th-century Wren church in Westminster, do indeed ring the famous tune on the day of its annual service commemorating the childhood rhyme. The association goes back to medieval times, when the churchyard of St Clement's reached the bank of the River Thames, and cargoes of fruit from overseas were transported through it. Since 1919, when a special service was organised to mark the re-hanging of the church bells, the church has hosted an annual Oranges and Lemons Service, in which children from the local primary school read poetry, sing, dance and play the handbells, each receiving an orange and a lemon to take home.
St Clement Danes, Westminster, London.

WOW LONDON

Women of the World is a global movement celebrating women and girls, with festivals taking place across the world all year round – and in London every March. It's all about events, performances, demonstrations, classes and debates in a fun, diverse and energetic atmosphere that's just as welcoming to men and boys as it is to women and girls of all ages and backgrounds.
Southbank Centre, London; thewowfoundation.com

GATESHEAD JAZZ

On the third weekend in March, this cutting-edge festival showcases the exciting melting pot of jazz, from dance music and Afro-beat to R&B and electronic music, featuring both acclaimed artists and rising stars.
Sage Gateshead; sagegateshead.com

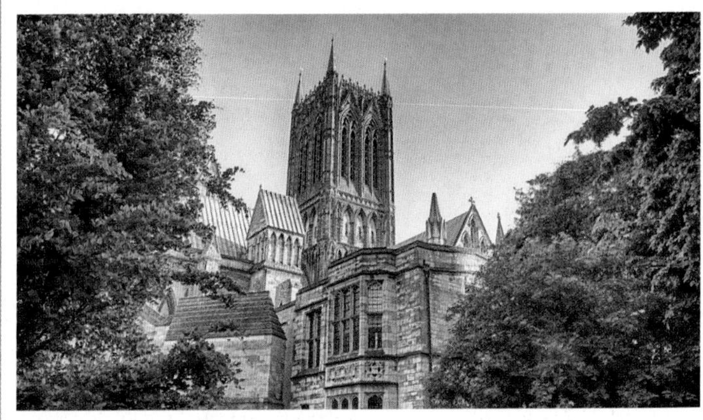
Cathedral Church of the Blessed Virgin Mary of Lincoln

DISCOVER LINCOLNSHIRE WEEKEND

Every March sees a weekend of free entry to many of the attractions in and around Lincoln, as well as other free activities and special offers. Highlights include free rides on Lincoln's open-top tour bus, free entry to Lincoln Cathedral and free guided tours of the city. For confirmation of dates and details, please visit the website nearer the time.
visitlincoln.com

Images: Getty, Shutterstock

BEAUTIFUL TOWN

CARTMEL

The village of Cartmel with Cartmel Priory Church at its centre

A cottage on Cartmel's riverbank

Cartmel Priory Gatehouse in summer

King's Arms, with the Priory Church behind

NESTLED in the rolling countryside of the Lake District Peninsula, the medieval village of Cartmel is renowned for its picturesque architecture of quaint cobbled streets, alleyways and collection of stone bridges that traverse the River Eea and its winding becks.

While the history of the village reaches back to the arrival of Lindisfarne monks around 680 AD, who took ownership of land in the area, it was during the 12th century that work began on a central landmark that stands in the centre of the village over 800 years later. Cartmel Priory was founded in 1189 by William Marshal, 1st Earl of Pembroke. The granting of an altar in one of its chapels helped the building survive Henry VIII's Dissolution of the Monasteries, alongside villagers arguing it was their parish church, as it remains to this day.

Today's visitors can explore its square belfry tower, view artworks by international sculptor Josefina de Vasconcellos, and see the bullet-pocked door known as Cromwell's Door after the Parliamentarian came under the fire of indignant villagers during the Civil War. Elsewhere, the priory's east window almost fills the entire wall and includes medieval glass fragments in a stunning display, while its antique choir stalls retain parts from 1450 and are still used for services.

Cartmel is known as one of the UK's best "foodie" villages, and perhaps its proudest boast is that it's the home of sticky toffee pudding, handmade in Cartmel's village shop for over 30 years. Indeed, the village caters for a wide range of culinary tastes with everything from regional cheeses, artisan breads, fine wines and locally brewed beer from a village-based micro-brewery.

All of these are housed within the courtyard setting of Unsworth Yard, and there is a choice of traditional tea rooms, including the Mallard Tea Shop. For fine diners and drinkers in search of a local brew, Cartmel's four pubs offer gastropub menus in historic settings, while award-winning chef Simon Rogan's Michelin-starred L'Enclume serves up epicurean adventures with local products.

For a spot of retail therapy, the square at the centre of Cartmel is the ideal starting point, offering a plethora of enticing inns, gift shops, an antiquarian book seller, coffee shops and interiors boutiques. From there, head down the many winding lanes to discover everything from hand-crafted gifts to antiques, art and chocolatiers.

RICHARD GINGER

Cartmel Priory Church

DON'T MISS

Cartmel Race Course

This rare attraction is one of the smallest in the country. The village's connections to horse racing reach back to the 15th century, although the first written account of the sport dates to 1856. The course hosts a popular calendar of steeplechase meetings, with its most valuable race, the Cumbria Crystal Cup, run during the July meeting.
cartmel-racecourse.co.uk

Hoker Hall and Gardens

Just under two miles from the village centre is Hoker Hall and Gardens, home to generations of the Cavendish family. The parkland surrounding the house extends to 200 acres grazed by a herd of fallow deer. The property houses an enviable collection of antiques and artworks, including Wedgwood Jasperware, 18th-century caricatures by Sir Joshua Reynolds, Chippendale and Hepplewhite furniture and William Morris fabrics.
holker.co.uk

Cartmel Village Shop

The owners began baking sticky toffee pudding in their kitchen over 30 years ago, winning a growing audience hungry for more. Today the pudding is still made by hand in small batches by the family-run business, with many ingredients sourced locally. Plaudits for the pud have come from the likes of Rick Stein, Jean-Christophe Novelli and Nigella Lawson.
cartmelvillageshop.co.uk

Images: Alamy, Shutterstock

GOON BUT NOT FORGOTTEN

Amanda Hodges celebrates *The Goon Show* which brought laughter into our homes from the 1950s

"IT was strange. Four fellows on a Sunday afternoon, getting slightly sozzled on brandy in between shows, made such an impact on the world of comedy."

And in such wryly bemused fashion did Harry Secombe (in his genial autobiography) describe the formative days of The Goons, the quartet comprising Secombe, Michael Bentine, Peter Sellers and the show's principal anchor, Spike Milligan. Alcohol, of course, was prohibited during rehearsals and recording, so the cast mixed brandy with milk to conceal any imbibing. In later episodes the catchphrase "round the back for the old brandy!" was used to announce the exit of a character or a musical interlude.

Their anarchic and surreal brand of creativity would make them legendary comedy pioneers in *The Goon Show*, which ran on the BBC Home Service from 1951-1960. Never forget though that for this innovative group the sheer enjoyment of their communal experience was always paramount. As effervescent Michael Bentine aptly expressed it, "If there was any hidden factor not known to the audience, it was that we were all smashed out of our heads with the sheer joy of living."

So how did it all begin? As the 1950s dawned, the cosy world of radio comedy had been galvanised by the long-running success of *ITMA* (*It's That Man Again*). The young Sellers was already working on radio, friends Secombe and Bentine had emerged from stints at London's infamous Windmill Theatre, and Milligan, also a friend of Secombe's, was writing jokes for comedian Derek Roy on BBC radio.

Many artists of the era gravitated to the Grafton Arms pub in Westminster where former army major Jimmy Grafton maintained dual roles of pub landlord and scriptwriter, providing a welcoming haven for fledgling entertainers. He would later be christened KOGVOS by The Goons, generally interpreted as meaning "King of the Goons, Voice of Sanity".

The four men had similarly quirky senses of humour and soon became friends, practising their jokes at the pub and using an early tape recorder to test out their zany comedy. Hearing some of this early taped material, helpful BBC

Still laughing: Secombe and Milligan at the launch of The Last Goon Show of All*, 1997*

Alamy, Getty Images, Shutterstock

From *The Jet-propelled Guided NAAFI* – Series 6, 24 January, 1956.

GRYTPYPE-THYNNE: *You illiterate swine. It's Moriarty; where are you?*

MORIARTY: *Here. In the piano.*

GRYTPYPE-THYNNE: *What the devil are you doing in there?*

MORIARTY: *I'm hidin'.*

GRYTPYPE-THYNNE: *Don't be silly, Haydn's been dead for years.*

The Goons cast with guest: (L-R) Spike Milligan, Peter Sellers, Ian Carmichael, Harry Secombe and Michael Bentine (C)

From *The Dreaded Batter-pudding Hurler* – Series 5, 12 October, 1954.

It's 1941. Minnie Bannister and her venerable friend Henry are out walking on the cliffs at night in Bexhill. She has been hit by an unidentified flying object. They light a match to see what it is . . .

[FX: striking match - bomb whistle - explosion]

HENRY CRUN: *...Curse... The British, the British!!!*

SEAGOON: *We tried using a candle, but it wasn't very bright and we daren't light it, so we waited for dawn, and there, in the light of the morning sun, we saw what had struck Miss Bannister. It was... A batter pudding!*

[Orchestra: dramatic chord]

HENRY CRUN: *It's still warm, Minnie.*

MINNIE BANNISTER: *Oh. Thank heaven, I hate cold batter pudding.*

producer Pat Dixon persuaded a rather reluctant BBC to give The Goons a platform, and in May 1951 their first show was, much to their chagrin, broadcast under the name of *Crazy People*, a name they disliked.

All of The Goons had experience within wartime ENSA (providing entertainment for the troops) and much of *The Goon Show*'s material was influenced by their time as ex-servicemen. Their disillusionment yielded disparagement of easy propaganda, spoofed authority figures and satirised (dubious) military heroism, here seen enshrined in the shape of a man like Major Bloodnok, one who'll take any bribe and shamelessly tell any falsehood to save face. The basis of The Goons' humour, Milligan once said, "is one man shouting gibberish in the face of authority, and proving by fabricated insanity that nothing could be as mad as what passes for ordinary living."

Looking back at these early days, Peter Sellers recalled, "We were young men with very strong and ambitious ideas. There used to be a form of euphoria, we were swept along and we swept people along with us. We were in another world." And it was clearly a world audiences enjoyed as the listening figures went from good to stratospheric, and another series of thirty-minute programmes was swiftly commissioned. The team's desire for it to be known as *The Goon Show* subsequently prevailed, although some executives never understood, persevering with what they called "The Go On Show", and Milligan maintained the name derived from a Popeye cartoon of the 1930s.

One of these early listeners was author Roger Wilmut, who wrote informative tome *The Goon Show Companion* in 1976, essential reading for fans. Wilmut says today, "I was at secondary school when The Goons hit their stride with the first series. I got to know about them from hearing the gags relayed (often garbled) by my schoolfriends. I took to listening and loved the off-beat humour, though my father – tired of hearing me repeat jokes and silly voices – forbade me to listen. This didn't stop me."

The sheer originality of the material created a devoted following, enthralled by The Goons' madcap weekly exploits (at a time when television was in its infancy) and BBC Transcription Services began broadcasting shows overseas. For the first two series, whilst Bentine was ensconced as madcap adventurer Dr Osric

>

From *The Spanish Suitcase* Series 5, 7 December, 1954.

MORIARTY: *I might say whoever planned the robbery must be a man of the highest intelligence, with the courage of a lion!*

SEAGOON: *So you suspect me?*

MORIARTY: *No.*

Down Among the Z Men: *(L-R) Peter Sellers, Carole Carr, Spike Milligan, Michael Bentine and Harry Secombe, 1952*

> Pureheart, whose actions never quite saw fulfilment, the show was essentially presented as a comedy-variety programme, with scripted comedy segments alternating with musical interludes, all introduced by a BBC announcer, initially Andrew Timothy and, subsequently, Wallace Greenslade. The episode *Dishonoured* in the fifth series began: "Here is a police message. A van-load of musical instruments was stolen this afternoon. It is believed to be having repercussions."

But after Bentine's amicable departure at the end of the second series (due to commitments and creative friction with Milligan), well before the show reached its peak popularity, under Peter Eton's tighter directorial attention all evolved into a more cohesive (if such a term ever applies to The Goons) narrative from the third series, often with Neddie Seagoon (Secombe) as the cash-strapped, guileless hero at its heart and invariably in peril.

Secombe, of the "cherubic countenance", as Jimmy Grafton remembered him, had a pleasant singing voice which was heard in many an episode during musical interludes. Secombe later happily recalled the atmosphere of creativity in London's old Camden Theatre: "It was like children being let out of school . . . you could always hear me, Peter or Spike giggling in the background."

The scripts, principally written by Milligan but also using co-writers Eric Sykes, Larry Stephens Jimmy Grafton and others, mixed fantastical plots with surreal humour, puns, catchphrases and an array of unusual sound effects. Plots were often bizarre romps through a variety of genres, from spoof spy drama, murder mystery or wartime caper. The first two series were unnamed, but from series three onwards this changed, with titles like *Ill Met by Goonlight* or the inspired insanity of *The Dreaded Batter-pudding Hurler of Bexhill-on-Sea.* On the surface all looked like sheer absurdity, but through the years many aspects of the British psyche were explored through the medium of their wacky style. Everything was performed at breakneck speed and acted as some sort of creative catharsis for those involved, as Sellers acknowledged: "That's why the show, for us, was such an enormous release and we used to pack so much energy in – we were just so keen to let people hear what was going on in our minds.

"I remember when we first met up," he continues. "Bentine, Harry, Spike and I had this feeling that we wanted to express ourselves in a sort of surrealistic form. We thought in cartoons, we thought in sketches, we thought of mad characters. The only way I can describe the form of humour we enjoyed is that we took any given situation and carried it to an illogical conclusion."

There were no hard and fast rules. As Milligan emphasised, "You could make characters do what you wanted because you were writing the script. You always win."

From *African Incident* Series 8, 30 Dec, 1957.

BLOODNOK: *What a strange sight it must have been. Me and the dusky beauty tango-ing through the dense jungle on foot.*

NATIVE WOMAN: *I only had eyes for him and he only had eyes for me.*

BLOODNOK: *That explains why we fell over a cliff.*

Milligan, Sellers and Secombe re-enact an earlier sketch with leeks, 1972

From *The Nadger Plague* Series 7, 18 October, 1956.

GRYTPYPE: *Oh, and landlord, we want a room with the walls facing inwards, a table laid with your best silver and napery . . .*

MORIARTY: *Yes, and a window overlooking our horse and a set of knotted sheets hanging therefrom.*

WILLIUM: *'Ere, wait a minute!*

MORIARTY: *What, mate?*

WILLIUM: *Sheets hanging out of the window?*

MORIARTY: *Yes, mate.*

WILLIUM: *I know what you're going to do, matey. The moment my back's turned that horse'll be up them sheets for a free night's kip.*

MORIARTY: *Curse it! Curse it! Curse it, Grytpype, he's guessed our plan.*

And clearly this non-stop stream of inventive ideas was all fuelled by Milligan's keen ingenuity, something that took a toll on his wellbeing. Milligan's mental health had long been fragile, and the constant demands on him as principal writer often proved too much. Commenting just before the reunion of *The Last Goon Show of All* in 1972, he said, "The pressure and the tension of keeping up the standard drove me mad." During series two it was necessary for him to spend weeks recovering in a psychiatric institution after a breakdown before he felt able to resume his workload.

The Goon Show was innovative in many respects, not least the way it subversively played with the medium of radio itself with characters exiting and entering doors in absurd fashion. And its zany sound effects, very innovative for the era, with frequent explosions, were notorious, many representing the infinite variety of options housed within Milligan's fertile imagination.

Just how eclectic his mind was is demonstrated in a lovely story that's so absurd it must be true. Milligan asked the canteen ladies at the Camden Theatre to make him some custard. Thinking he must have stomach trouble they kindly made him some fresh. Imagine their horror when, after accepting it with thanks, he duly poured it into his sock in order to test out his theory about its potential squelching effect.

It proved disappointing, but there were few limits to Milligan's mind and nothing seemed elusive. One of the lines in a script read, "Sound effect of two lions walking away, bumping against each other. If you can't get two lions, two hippos will do!" More feasibly, one of the show's most familiar devices, enhanced by the new magnetic tape being used, was the blood-curdling range of sounds designed to conjure Bloodnok's volatile digestive system.

Many Goon expressions became catchphrases. "The dreaded lurgi", used to denote an unspecified condition, from a 1954 show even entered the vernacular. Amongst many others there was Grytpype-Thynne offering colleagues strange objects rather than cigarettes: namely, Neddie Seagoon is asked, "Have a gorilla?" with the reply: "No, thanks, I'm trying to give them up." And Secombe's benign Neddie Seagoon would yodel "Needle-nardle-noo" at any opportunity.

For people like Milligan and Sellers, who often found reality too prosaic, the realm of The Goons provided the perfect working environment. Sellers repeatedly said, "They really were my happiest days, those Sundays when we did *The Goon Show* . . . It was the happiest professional period of my life." As Milligan's former manager and close friend Norma Farnes remarks, "Spike and Peter had many traits in common . . . they blurred the margins of fantasy and reality, loved pranks and shared an amazing amount of talent."

Roger Wilmut (of *The Goon Show Companion*) affirms, "Of course, Milligan, as the writer, with assistance from others, was the prime mover, but his ability to create believable odd characters closely matched Sellers's. Apart from actual jokes, the characters themselves were much more strongly drawn than the eccentrics >

Sellers, Secombe and Milligan perform for a televised radio production, 1968

Down Among the Z Men (which saw all but Secombe reprising their *The Goon Show* personas) and also had hit songs in the Fifties with nonsense numbers like the popular *Ying Tong Song*.

In the early Sixties *The Telegoons* – 15-minute puppet shows using revamped *The Goon Show* scripts – appeared on BBC TV. The Goons numbered amongst their legion of fans Prince Charles and the fledgling Beatles, with John Lennon being particularly receptive to their brand of dissident anarchy.

> in other comedy shows."

And who were these memorable characters? They were a motley assortment greatly benefiting from Milligan's natural ingenuity and Sellers's inimitable vocal versatility. This encompassed the high-pitched squeaks of Sellers's young scout Bluebottle, for ever complaining he'd been "deaded" or reading out stage directions ("Audience applause. Not a sausage"), the smooth tones of suave villain Hercules Grytpype-Thynne saying, "You silly, twisted boy, you" to the hapless Seagoon and opportunistic and flatulent swine Major Bloodnok. Milligan voiced French criminal Jim Moriarty, female character Minnie Bannister ("We'll all be murdered in our beds") and, of course, everyman Eccles, "the famous Eccles", as he'd proudly assert.

In his early radio forays Milligan had developed an idiot voice later used for the simple soul of Eccles. Milligan recognised much of himself in his distinctive creation: "Eccles was really the innocent creature that I was – the one that didn't want to cause any offence and loved simplicity, which I do. Yes, Eccles was the essential me."

Reviewing The Goons' legacy today, author Roger Wilmut says, "They were more off-the-wall than other comedy shows, which were mostly fairly cosy like *Life with the Lyons*, with Hancock being the best. They built on the legacy of *ITMA* – quite off-the-wall for its time – and though the first few series were a bit rough, they honed it into a form which was subversive and pushed the limits of comedy and surrealist logic. This appealed to many people in a fairly constrained era."

And his personal choice of episode? "My favourite would be *Call of the West* from the penultimate series – the ninth – where everything came gloriously together. The short remaining series showed it beginning to fall apart."

After so many years of intense commitment, Milligan would end the show after the tenth series. The final episode was entitled *The Last Smoking Seagoon* and went out on 28 January, 1960.

Broadcast internationally from 1954, The Goons made the film

Script co-writer Eric Sykes once said that their impact for him was dramatic: "The first time I heard a Goon Show on the radio, it was like walking through clear air after being stranded in a fog."

Modern-day comedians such as Eddie Izzard have also paid homage to the way in which The Goons shook up the comedy world and left it infinitely improved in their wake. And their influence on the embryonic Monty Python team proved palpable, with Terry Jones and John Cleese both big fans.

Cleese is quoted as saying, "It was more a spirit that was passed on, rather than any particular technique. The point is that once somebody has crossed a barrier and done something that has never been done before, it is terribly easy for everybody else to cross it."

This The Goons achieved with unmistakable brilliance.

FURTHER READING

Memories of Milligan, Norma Farnes (4th Estate, 2010)
The Goons, The Story, Norma Farnes (Ed) (Virgin Books, 1997)
The Goon Show Companion, Roger Wilmut and Jimmy Grafton (Robson Books, 1976)
The Life and Death of Peter Sellers, Roger Lewis (Arrow Books, 2004)
The Reluctant Jester, Michael Bentine (Corgi, 1992)
An Entertaining Life, Harry Secombe (Robson Books, 2001)
Spike, An Intimate Memoir, Norma Farnes (Fourth Estate, 2003)

The iconic suspension bridge, but where?

Antony Gormley's sculptures look out from?

Great art at Pallant House in which city?

THE GREAT GEOGRAPHY QUIZ

Test your knowledge of these well-known places in England . . .

1. The Vindolanda writing tablets, one of Britain's top treasures, were discovered in which county?

2. In which county is the National Horseracing Museum?

3. Where will you find Isambard Kingdom Brunel's Clifton Suspension Bridge?

4. The Magic Roundabout is a ring junction consisting of five mini-roundabouts in a circle around a sixth roundabout. In which town and county is it?

5. Antony Gormley's 100 figures staring out to sea, Another Place, are situated on which beach?

6. Cambridgeshire is made up of two previous historic counties. What were they?

7. Where will you find the Pallant House Gallery, which has a large collection of British art from 1900 onwards?

8. Which two rivers join to become the River Mersey, and in which town does this happen?

When was this art gallery built, and where?

9. They've been sketched by Turner and visited by Wordsworth, but in which National Park are Aysgarth Falls?

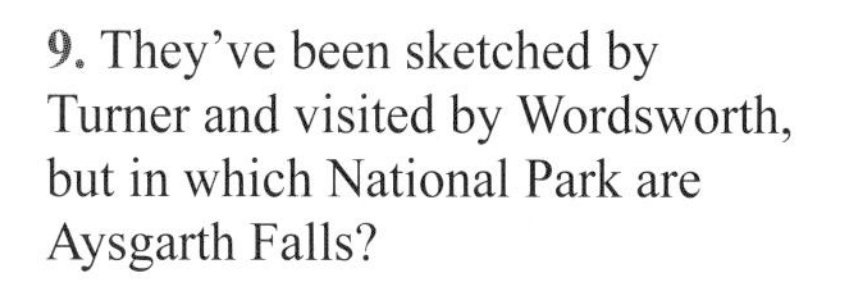

10. Virginia Woolf and her husband lived in Monk's House, Rodmell, from 1919 until her death in 1941. In which county will you find it?

11. The BALTIC centre for Contemporary Art was built in which city, and which year?

12. Alfred Wainwright mapped out walks in which National Park?

13. In which county is the National Trust Museum of Childhood?

14. Which cathedral was rebuilt within the ruins of the old one which was bombed during World War II? >

The "little Switzerland of England" is where?

The sleeping giant in the Lost Gardens of Heligan in which county?

> **15.** Which city was designated England's first UNESCO City of Literature in 2012?

16. George Tupper struck a buried fountain with his plough in 1811, which led to some of the most spectacular mosaics being discovered. In which county is Bignor Roman Villa?

17. Which county town describes Cardinal Wolsey as its most famous son?

18. This town in Northumberland hosted its own Olympic Games, which mainly consisted of wrestling and athletics, from the early 1870s until 1958. What is it called?

19. Which town in which county celebrated the bicentenary of the birth of British tourism in 2020?

20. The River Lea, the London river that empties into the Thames, starts in which home county?

21. In which county is the Prime Minister's country residence, Chequers?

22. The Battle of Sedgemoor is often touted as the last pitched battle in England. In which county did it take place?

23. The last proper punishment by ducking stool inflicted on Jenny Pipes in 1809 was carried out in which English market town?

24. The UK's largest aquarium boasts some 4,000 sea creatures, including sharks, turtles and eagle rays. In which city will you find it?

25. Benedictine monks established a swannery here, and now the 25-acre site is a base for more than 600 swans and the only managed colony of nesting mute swans in the world. Where will you find it?

26. The tallest gravity fountain in the world can be found at a Jacobean manor house, Stanway. Which spa town is it near?

27. The Silk Museum, telling the story of the surrounding region's silk history, is in which town?

28. Europe's largest garden restoration at Heligan has resulted in a spectacular 200-acre Victorian mix of pleasure and productive gardens. In which county will you find it?

29. The sculpture known as The Angel of the South is made from willow. In which county does she stand?

30. In which town will you find the Cromwell Museum, housed in Oliver Cromwell's former school?

31. Cartoonist Tim Hunkin's machines including "Whack A Banker" and "The Bathyscape" are located on which pier?

32. The Church of St Andrew's, the oldest wooden church in the

Where will you find Derek Jarman's Prospect Cottage?

It's the home of chocolate and celebrates with a festival, where is it?

A Regency gem of a theatre, but where?

world, dating back to 1060, is located in which village and county?

33. The Turner Contemporary gallery is in which seaside resort in which county?

34. Sculptor Henry Moore moved to Hoglands with his wife Irina and stayed for the rest of their lives. In which county is Hoglands?

35. The twin towns of Lynton and Lynmouth were described by the Victorians as "the little Switzerland of England". In which county will you find them?

36. Billed as "the most treasured Austen site in the world", where will you find Jane Austen's House Museum, where you can see her letters and where she wrote her much-loved novels?

37. Which city, where Joseph Rowntree set up his confectionery business, has an annual festival of chocolate?

38. Sunderland Point is situated at the mouth of which river?

39. Artist Derek Jarman's garden at Prospect Cottage was in the news recently as funds were raised to rescue it. The cottage is near which nuclear power station in which county?

40. The Theatre Royal, a Regency gem owned by the National Trust, is located in which market town?

41. John Betjeman said he had been "lifted up to Heaven" on the steepest cliff railway in inland Britain, which is in which Shropshire town?

This was MP Nancy Astor's home, but in which county?

42. Nancy Astor was England's first female MP. In which county was her home, which is now a high-end hotel?

43. In which dockyard in which county was HMS Victory built and launched from in 1765?

44. In which National Park will you find the Hole of Horcum, said to have been formed by a soil-throwing sea giant?

45. Which county has the former Westmorland been part of since 1974?

46. In 2021 The Open golf championship returns to the Royal St George's course. Which town and county is it in?

47. The Alum Bay cliffs are on the Isle of Wight. In which year did the Isle of Wight become an independent county, and from which other did it break away?

48. Old Harry Rocks are on the south coast, but which is the nearest town to this rock formation?

49. The French Lieutenant's Woman walked along The Cobb, in which quaint Dorset town?

50. It's a harbour that attracted artists such as Stanhope Forbes and Norman Garstin, whose realistic style was fashionable at the end of the 19th century. Where is it?

To see how you got on, turn to page 106 for answers.

ENGLAND'S PRIDE

Fiona Stapley, Editor of the Good Pub Guide, shares her pick of our nation's pubs. They're all worth crossing ploughed fields to get to – though, luckily, there's no need . . .

A former coaching inn, The Bell dates back to the 15th century and is nestled in the lovely historic village of Horndon-on-the-Hill.

"People may be surprised to find this small rural village so close to the M25," says Joanne Butler – general manager of 37 years.

The heavily beamed, panelled bar has high-backed antique settles and benches, rugs on flagstones, polished oak floorboards and an open log fire. Curiously, there is a collection of ossified hot-cross buns hanging along a beam in the saloon bar – the first was put there in 1906 to mark the day (a Good Friday) that Jack Turnell became licensee and a bun has been added every year since!

"If I had to sum up the pub in three words, I'd say welcoming, comforting and buzzing," says Joanne. "It breathes life into our community and is a place people want to visit to feel happy, comforted and recognised. People come together from a wide range of backgrounds but with a common love of good food and drink served by friendly people."

Horndon-on-the-Hill, Stanford-le-Hope, Essex SS17 8LD. 01375 642463; bell-inn.co.uk

Hot-cross buns hang in the saloon bar

Home to outstanding food . . .

Excellent food is always a draw, but when it's also cooked by the convivial landlord, that's the proverbial icing on the cake.

"We make everything on site, from the butter and bread at the start of your meal to the chocolates at the end," says Rob Allcock who runs the pub with wife, Liz. The pub has its own smokehouse and is famous for its smoked salmon.

"The outstanding fish is from Wester Ross in Scotland and is hand reared and hand fed – it's the only company I know of that still does this."

Rob is currently researching recipes for traditional Wiltshire cheese that hasn't been made for 100 years. During the Covid-19 crisis, he turned the pub into a bakery, making sourdough loaves and bath buns.

"We care so much about the food we serve to our customers . . . I don't get up in the morning to make money, I get up to cook for them."

Bradford-on-Avon BA15 2SB. 01225 864450; thelongsarms.com

The inn lies in an Area of Outstanding Natural Beauty

Open fireplaces and cosy armchairs

The well-stocked shop

Reports on this elegant manor house remain as warm and enthusiastic as ever – it's a very special place. Set high on the banks of the River Hodder, there are spectacular views from the inn down the valley into the heart of the Forest of Bowland, which is surrounded by fells and an Area of Outstanding Natural Beauty. The riverside bar and adjacent terrace make the most of this outlook. You can also fish for trout, salmon and sea trout along this stretch of the river. Picnic hampers available on request!

There's a long-standing royal connection here, as both the forest and inn form part of the Duchy of Lancaster, and even HM the Queen and The Duke of Edinburgh visited the pub in 2006, enjoying the Queen's 80th-birthday celebratory lunch before continuing their tour of the estate.

"In the 1300s, the building was lived in by the keepers of the Royal forest," says Louise Bowman, who co-owns the pub with her husband, Charles. "It wasn't until comparatively recently, during the 1700s, that it was transformed into a resting place where travellers en route to or from Lancaster could safely stay."

The lovely bedrooms (several have open fires) are individually furnished and have beautifully restored bathrooms. The civilised bar rooms have handsome old wood furnishings and sonorous clocks, set off beautifully against powder-blue walls hung with big, appealing prints. The main bar has roaring log fires and you'll find a selection of newspapers and magazines, local maps and guidebooks. There's a piano for anyone who wants to tinkle the ivories, and board games to while away an afternoon.

"The Inn at Whitewell is many things to many people," continues Louise. "Locals who come to eat and drink with us, customers who stay on a regular basis from all over the UK as well as further afield, couples who get married with us, walkers and ramblers, fishermen and many shooting parties. Many of our brilliant staff have been with us for a very long time – our general manager has been working in the inn since he started washing up at fourteen, and our head chef has been with us for twenty-five years." It's a place you want to stay . . .

Near Clitheroe, Lancashire BB7 3AT. 01200 448222; innatwhitewell.com

A wood-burning stove keeps the bar cosy

Pretty much faultless in all aspects . . .

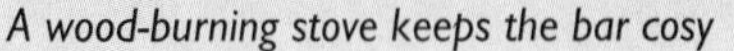

Lucky Cambridgeshire. This pub is pretty much faultless in all aspects, starting with its location in the beautiful village of Hemingford Grey, 100 metres from the Great Ouse river. One feature we particularly like in a place that serves first-class food is that they've sensibly kept their public bar for drinking only, and Adnams Southwold, Brewsters Hophead and Oldershaw Grantham Stout are all on handpump.

From the other drinks on offer, two stand out in particular: Cromwell Cider, made by Tony and Sarah Hobbs who have orchards on the outskirts of the village, and Roundwood Gin, which is made down the road in Huntington from elderflower and elderberries found in the woodlands that surround the distillery.

Move through to the stylishly rustic restaurant (you must book to be sure of a table) and you're in for exceptional dining. The Cock is famous for two dishes which they've offered for more than 20 years: their duck parcel – filo pastry filled with shredded confit duck in a hoi sin sauce – and their homemade sausages: choose three or four different types plus a mash and sauce to go with it.

Outside on the terrace, there are seats and tables among stone troughs and flowers and, in the neat garden, pretty hanging baskets.

47 High Street, Hemingford Grey, Huntingdon PE28 9BJ. 01480 463609; the thecockhemingford.co.uk

Yorkshire's Denton Hall was once home to the Wyvill family

This former farmhouse in the Yorkshire Dales, now a well-established pub, hotel and restaurant, couldn't be in safer hands. Current owners the Stevens family have not only lovingly looked after it for the past 10 years, but also have more than 50 years in the hospitality industry. You could say the business runs through landlord and chef Nigel Stevens's veins; he grew up in pubs run by his late father, Roger, and mother Terry, across the north-east and North Yorkshire, including several in Wensleydale.

Inside you'll find two bar areas, one with a finely worked plaster ceiling with the Wyvill family's coat of arms, and the second with a model train on a railway track running around the room. Outside, large wooden benches under white parasols are ready for outdoor dining. There are comfortable bedrooms which make a great base for exploring the area (Constable Burton Hall is opposite), and you'll get a generous breakfast to set you up before you go.

Constable Burton, Leyburn, Yorkshire DL8 5LH. 01677 450581; thewyvillarms.co.uk

The hard-working team

Dish of the day: lightly smoked trout

You're guaranteed a restful night's sleep here

"If the Olive Branch makes people feel special and come back, we have done our job," says Ben Jones, co-owner and landlord of this brilliant inn since 1999, "but when they tell us it holds an extra-special place in their hearts, that makes us feel very proud."

Based in the pretty village of Clipsham, in England's smallest county, this pub's story goes back to 1880 when three farm labourers' cottages were opened up and connected to make the local ale house.

The conversion left various small and attractive bar rooms and today you'll find these furnished with rustic pieces, an interesting mix of pictures (some by local artists), candles on tables and a cosy log fire in a stone inglenook fireplace.

There's an exciting choice of beers and wines, including several British and Continental bottled beers, but the real stars are the cocktails, made using the pub's own seasonal ingredients from the kitchen garden. Lots and lots of things are made in house – jams, chutneys, pickles, ketchups, ice-creams – or sourced from award-winning producers: bread from Hambleton Bakery, pork pies from Price & Fretwell butchers and the cured meats of Melton Charcuterie. Events are also the order of the day.

"We do wine, butchery and bakery tutored masterclasses and cookery demonstrations," says Ben.

Outside, tables, chairs and big plant pots sit on a pretty little terrace, with seating on the neat lawn, sheltered in the crook of two low buildings, and across the road from the main pub a renovated Georgian property, Beech House, houses individually decorated, restful bedrooms.

Main Street, Clipsham, Rutland LE15 7SH. 01780 410 355; theolivebranchpub.com

Organised county by county and only including the best pubs , The Good Pub Guide is Britain's bestselling travel guide. The 2021 edition will be published later this year.

I Love to See the Summer Beaming Forth

By John Clare

I love to see the summer beaming forth
And white wool sack clouds sailing to the north
I love to see the wild flowers come again
And Mare blobs stain with gold the meadow drain,
And water lilies whiten on the floods
Where reed clumps rustle like a wind shook wood
Where, from her hiding place, the Moor Hen pushes
And seeks her flag nest floating in bull rushes
I like the willow leaning half way o'er
The clear deep lake to stand upon its shore
I love the hay grass when the flower head swings
To summer winds and insects happy wings
That sport about the meadow the bright day
And see bright beetles in the clear lake play

Images: Getty

A traditional wildflower hay meadow in full bloom in Hawes, Yorkshire

SPRING TO SUMMER

Events including the Chelsea Flower Show and cheese rolling, plus a visit to Polperro and the history of Blackpool Pleasure Beach >

SPRING TO SUMMER

Revel in a festival, cheer at the races or dance your way through May; we're in for one heck of a summer, says Katherine Sorrell

APRIL 2021

EARTH DAY

Every year on 22 April, Earth Day marks the anniversary of the birth of the modern environmental movement in 1970. As part of a global initiative to help protect and restore the planet, there are actions happening all over England, from beach cleans to teach-ins, which anyone is welcome to join.
earthday.org

SHAKESPEARE'S BIRTHDAY CELEBRATIONS

Shakespeare's birthday is marked every year in his hometown of Stratford-upon-Avon on a weekend close to 23 April. Highlights include a parade led by Will Shakespeare himself, folk dancing and street entertainment, and the laying of a wreath at Holy Trinity Church where the playwright is buried. The party continues at each of Shakespeare's family homes with a range of special events.
Stratford-upon-Avon; shakespeare.org.uk

MALDON MUD RACE

This mad, mud bath/charity fund-raiser takes place on a Sunday in late April or early May. It has been going since the 1970s and, as with many such things, its origins lie in a bright idea in the local pub. Described as "fun with a competitive edge", it draws crowds in the tens of thousands to watch competitors, often in fancy-dress, make their way through the deep, thick mud of the Blackwater Estuary and back, on a 400-metre-long course. Entry to watch in Promenade Park is by donation, huge TV screens capture every moment and there are stalls, refreshments, activities and entertainment during the day.
Maldon, Essex; maldonmudrace.com

TREVITHICK DAY

Engineer and inventor Richard Trevithick constructed the world's first steam railway locomotive, and each year on the last Saturday of April his life and work, as well as the mining history of the area, is celebrated with a festival of free street entertainment in the Cornish town of Camborne. In addition to music of all styles, food, stalls and a flower festival, there are two special dances during the day, the first performed by local children in the costume of bal maidens and miners, and the second by adults dressed in the Cornish colours of black and gold. These are followed by an impressive parade of vintage steam vehicles – probably the largest array of steam engines in the world to proceed through a town.
Camborne, Cornwall; visitcornwall.com

A replica of Richard Trevithick's Puffing Devil steam locomotive on Trevithick day, which is always the last Saturday in April in Camborne

The annual university boat-race, circa 1878

THE BOAT RACE

The annual contest between rowing crews from Oxford and Cambridge universities takes place close to Easter each year on the River Thames between Putney and Mortlake. There are places to watch the race for free along the full length of the course, with some of the best viewpoints being Putney Embankment near the start, Chiswick Pier in the centre and, for the final stages of the race, Dukes Meadow, a large park between Chiswick bridge and Barnes bridge.
www.theboatrace.org

THE TUDOR PULL

Usually taking place on a Sunday in April or May, the Tudor Pull is a ceremonial event in which traditional Thames cutters and other craft escort the Thames Royal Shallop Jubilant and Gloriana, the Queen's rowbarge, from Hampton Court Palace to the Tower of London, delivering a ceremonial token to the governor of the tower for safekeeping. Expect a visual spectacle with much pageantry, flags and colourful regalia.
pla.co.uk/Events/The-Tudor-Pull

FRITILLARY SUNDAY

The delicate snake's head fritillary flower once carpeted the wet meadows of England; now it is a rare sight, found only in a handful of places in southern England and the Midlands. One such site is Ducklington Mead, which is the only place in England where it is possible to walk among the flowers – for just one day a year. On Fritillary Sunday the ten-acre meadow is opened to the public, who may also enjoy food, drink, activities, folk dancing, handbell ringing and other music, with all proceeds going to Ducklington Church.
Ducklington, Oxfordshire; ducklingtonchurch.org.uk

CUCKOO DAY

The cuckoo fair in Heathfield, East Sussex, is said to date back to 1315, when Dame Heffle (the old name for Heathfield) used to arrive at a gypsy market and release cuckoos to announce the start of spring. These days cuckoos are rather hard to come by, so racing

The Grand National at Aintree, a highlight of the racing calendar

THE GRAND NATIONAL

Watched by millions around the world, the Grand National is best known for the four-mile steeplechase that is the ultimate challenge in jump racing. It is, in fact, a three-day festival, with the first day, Liverpool's Day, a relaxed day of racing and entertainment. The second day, Ladies' Day, focuses on fashion – look for some extraordinary hats! In the exciting finale of the Grand National itself, 40 horses and riders jump 30 notoriously difficult fences over two laps of the Aintree course.
Aintree Racecourse, Merseyside; thejockeyclub.co.uk

>

> pigeons are used instead. The day also includes craft stalls, food and drink, displays and performances, vintage cars, a fun fair and a dog show raising money for Demelza Hospice Care for Children.

Meanwhile, at Marsden, West Yorkshire, the Cuckoo Day celebration (traditionally taking place on the last Saturday of April) encompasses artistic workshops, a craft fair, maypole and Morris dancing as well as the highlight, a village procession led by a giant wicker-and-paper cuckoo. In days gone by, the people of the village reputedly built a huge wall to try to prolong the cuckoo's visit. There's also a cuckoo fair at Downtown, Wiltshire, on the Saturday of the first May bank holiday, offering demonstrations of rural crafts, Punch and Judy, fairground stalls and a produce market. **facebook.com/pg/hefflecuckoofair1315; facebook.com/pg/MarsdenCuckoo; cuckoofair.co.uk**

LONDON COFFEE FESTIVAL

If you can't start your day without a cup of joe, then you won't want to miss this celebration of London's vibrant coffee scene, featuring more than 250 artisan coffee and gourmet food stalls, tastings and demonstrations from world-class baristas, interactive workshops, street food, coffee-based cocktails, live music, DJs, art exhibitions and more. It's the centrepiece of UK Coffee Week which raises funds for Project Waterfall, a charity working to bring clean water, sanitation and education to coffee-growing communities across the world. **The Truman Brewery, East London; londoncoffeefestival.com**

ST GEORGE'S DAY

Morris men in Leadenhall Market, London

A feast day of St George has been celebrated in England for hundreds of years on 23 April, possibly the date of our patron saint's martyrdom. Events include an English Heritage festival at Wrest Park, Bedfordshire, billed as the biggest, most action-packed St George's Day celebration in the country, with performances, games, battles and, of course, a showdown between St George and his fiery dragon. Salisbury is also known for its family-friendly event that includes Morris dancing, live music, fair rides, free workshops and parades. In London there's a free celebration in Trafalgar Square where the focus is on live entertainment and a food market; and Leadenhall Market hosts Morris dancers and a brass band in its annual extravaganza. **english-heritage.org.uk; london.gov.uk; visitwiltshire.co.uk/salisbury; leadenhallmarket.co.uk**

Our bluebell woods are a delightful April/May experience

BLUEBELL WALKS

Did you know that half of the world's population of bluebells flowers in the UK? A tranquil walk through an ancient woodland carpeted with beautifully coloured and scented bluebells is a wonderful springtime experience. On the last Sunday in April, for example, Combermere Abbey in Cheshire opens for its two-mile bluebell walk – one of the only times of the year when it is possible to tour its gardens, which also include walled gardens with a restored Edwardian glasshouse and the only fruit tree maze in the world. The Bluebell Day at Hatchlands Park, Surrey, supports the National Gardens Scheme and promises a riot of colour in Little Wix Wood, a quiet patch of ancient semi-natural woodland that was first recorded in the Chertsey Chronicles during the 13th century. Another much-loved walk is the Arlington Bluebell Walk and Farm Trail – actually seven walks over three working farms with vistas of bluebells that have established over centuries. The National Trust and the Woodland Trust have lists of bluebell walks around the country. **combermereabbey.co.uk; nationaltrust.org.uk; bluebellwalk.co.uk; woodlandtrust.org.uk**

MAY 2021

ROYAL WINDSOR HORSE SHOW

Taking place in the grounds of Windsor Castle, the show has top equestrian sport on offer, including international show jumping and dressage plus more than 140 showing classes. There are displays and music from military troops and bands, the much-loved Shetland pony Grand National and a pageant with music.

Windsor, Berkshire; rwhs.co.uk

GLYNDEBOURNE FESTIVAL

The season of world-class opera in the heart of the Sussex countryside begins in May. The Festival has a tradition of formal dress, with audiences enjoying the 90-minute interval with a picnic in the gardens.

Lewes, East Sussex; glyndebourne.com

DOGFEST

The ultimate dogs' day out, this festival is all about the unconditional love between man (or woman) and their four-legged friend. Enjoy demonstrations and displays by talented canines, give your pooch a go at flyball, hay-bale jumping or obedience. Or enter them into a novelty class such as waggiest tail, golden oldie or best paw shaker. Dogfest South takes place at Knebworth House, Hertfordshire, on 8 and 9 May, with two further festivals in Tatton Park, Cheshire and Ashton Court, Bristol, in June.

dog-fest.co.uk

Shih Tzus at Dogfest, Knebworth Park

HM the Queen is a regular visitor to the Chelsea Flower Show

THE ELGAR FESTIVAL

Held annually during the weekend closest to Elgar's birthday (2 June, 1857), this four-day musical celebration of our greatest composer is based in and around his home town of Worcester, and combines an ambitious programme of concerts, workshops and recitals with plays, exhibits, talks and community projects and an array of guest artists.

Worcester and nearby, Worcestershire; elgarfestival.org

LICHFIELD BOWER

Not many community festivals can claim a history all the way back to 1145. Lichfield's spring bank holiday Monday event, however, dates back to Henry II's demands for an annual muster of fighting men. Back then, they were assembled before magistrates at a "bower house" decorated with laurel and lilac, given free beef and wine and then paraded around the city accompanied by Lichfield's Morris dancers. These days, there's still a procession, now with bands and floats, plus a humorous "court of array", fairground attractions, arts and crafts, food and market stalls and live music.

Lichfield, Staffordshire; lichfieldbower.co.uk

RHS CHELSEA FLOWER SHOW

The world's most prestigious flower show brings together extraordinary show gardens and some of the best international nurseries and growers over five days in Chelsea. Get expert advice, spot emerging trends, find out about the science behind horticulture and indulge in some garden-related retail therapy as you admire incredible horticultural creativity.

Royal Hospital Chelsea, London; rhs.org.uk

BRIGHTON FESTIVALS

Head down to the south coast for festivals in and around Brighton during May. There's Brighton Festival itself, a three-week celebration of music, theatre, dance, circus, art, film and literature that's run since 1967; Brighton Fringe, an open-access festival meaning anyone can take part, so anything goes (!); Artist Open Houses, in which more than 1000 artists exhibit their work; The Great Escape, the festival for new music; and Foodies Festival, the UK's largest celebration of food and drink. Nearby stately home Charleston looks at art, literature, politics and ideas past and present, with an eye to challenging the status quo and daring to imagine society differently – just as the Bloomsbury group did around the Charleston dining-room table 100 years ago.

Brighton and nearby, East Sussex; visitbrighton.com

Bunches of watercress at Alresford's annual festival. The town was built from the riches of this superfood

THE ALRESFORD WATERCRESS FESTIVAL

Watercress takes centre stage in the town of Alresford on the third Sunday of May each year, marking the start of the new UK season of the popular peppery superfood. The Georgian market town was built from the riches of the watercress industry, even boasting its own steam railway nicknamed the Watercress Line. In its Victorian heyday it carried the freshly harvested watercress to London markets; today's festival-goers can travel to the event the same way on a park and ride scheme from nearby Ropley. A huge street festival includes food and craft stalls, live music, cookery demonstrations, children's activities and a parade in which the Watercress King and Queen dispense freshly harvested watercress. The *pièce de résistance* is The World Watercress Eating Championships. The world record for an 85g bag? Just 32 seconds.

Alresford, Hampshire; watercressfestival.org

> BATH FESTIVALS

Bath's flagship festival of music and literature brings world-class artists and authors to the city and is accompanied by a Fringe Festival with myriad art forms. It ends with an extravaganza of music, food and fun.

Bath, Somerset; bathfestivals.org.uk

TORTOISE FAIR

A summer afternoon of jolly japes and . . . tortoise racing? Yes, you did read that correctly. It all began as a gentlemanly challenge issued by Corpus Christi College students to their counterparts in Oriel, and now it's a firm fixture in the Oxford year, usually held on the sixth Sunday of the Trinity term. Live music, entertainment and refreshments accompany the main reptilian race.

Corpus Christi College, Oxford; corpusjcr.org/clubs-and-societies/tortoise-fair/

A competitor from earlier times

ENGLISH WINE & FOOD FESTIVAL

Taste, compare and buy award-winning English wines from producers in the Thames and Chilterns regions. Meet winemakers, growers and other experts, learn more about the grape varieties that do well in our climate, walk around the vineyard and enjoy pairing the crisp, fruity wines with freshly made food. Cheers!

Brightwell Vineyard, Wallingford, Oxfordshire; englishwineandfoodfestival.co.uk

CRAB & LOBSTER FESTIVAL

Two of Norfolk's popular seaside destinations, Cromer and Sheringham, get together to enjoy food, art and music in this lively celebration of their seafaring heritage and fishing communities. The three-day event kicks off with a variety concert and features celebrity and local chefs cooking lobster, crab and other favourite recipes, as well as the ultimate crab sandwich competition, sea shanties, crab-pot making and heaps of other entertainment. The whole family can take part in the World Pier Crabbing Championships and there's even a fringe festival – of gardening.

Cromer, Norfolk; crabandlobsterfestival.co.uk

DECORATIVE LIVING FAIR

The annual one-day Decorative Living Fair takes place at Eridge Park, a country estate on the borders of Kent and Sussex. It has been run since 2006 by textile designer Caroline Zoob and antiques dealer Henrietta "Hetty" Purbrick. Bringing together a wide variety of dealers in antique, vintage and contemporary decorative goods, the fair has a dedicated following and a relaxed, convivial atmosphere.

Eridge Park, Kent; decorativelivingfair.co.uk

COOPERS HILL CHEESE ROLLING

What do you get when you combine the spring bank holiday, a very steep hill and a wheel of Double Gloucester? The answer is this world-famous, somewhat bizarre and really quite dangerous event. The cheese reaches speeds of more than 70mph (and it's not unheard of for entrants to be hospitalised) but if you're the winner you get to keep it! Enter very much at your own risk.

Brockworth, Gloucestershire; officialcheeserolling.com

MAY DANCING

Dancing is strongly associated with this month, and Morris groups all over England "dance in the May" with a dawn jig. Later on, there may well be maypole dancing or a May fair – though, these days, the latter are more often found on a bank holiday weekend. Another ancient feature is the Jack in the Green, a man encased in a tall framework of foliage and flowers who is a traditional participant in celebrations and dances, sometimes accompanied by attendants called Bogies. The Knutsford Jack is probably the oldest continual annual Jack in the Green, but there are around 20 up and down the country, including Deptford in London, Bristol, Hastings and Whitstable. Another character that can sometimes be seen dancing through towns on May Day or as part of a festival is the Hobby Horse, which performs antics with a folk band as part of a tradition dating back to the 18th century. The Minehead hobby horse takes to the streets on the first three days of the month, while in Padstow there are two 'Obby 'Osses which parade around the town. A dance takes place in Helston, Cornwall, as part of its annual Flora Day – the Furry Dance, in which 80 local couples, dressed in top hat and tails or evening dress, dance through the streets, entering selected houses and shops to drive out the darkness of winter and bring in the light of spring. **themorrisring.org; thecompanyofthegreenman.com; swheritage.org.uk; padstowobbyoss.wordpress.com; helstonfloraday.org.uk**

Jack in the Green (aka Jack o' the Green) Festivities, from an old print. May dancing is traditionally associated with May Day

JUNE 2021

EPSOM DERBY

One of our great national sporting events, the Derby is a flat horse race run over a mile and a half and open to three-year-old colts and fillies. Alongside the racing, expect lots of people dressed up to the nines, plenty of picnics, live music and all sorts of other entertainment from skydivers to celebrity DJ parties.
Epsom Downs Racecourse, Surrey; thejockeyclub.co.uk

ROYAL ACADEMY SUMMER EXHIBITION

Anyone can enter their works of art into the Royal Academy's summer exhibition, which features new and recent art created by everyone from emerging artists to the biggest names in contemporary art and architecture. Many of the galleries in Burlington House are hung densely, while some are dedicated to a single artist. Others feature film, photography or installations.
Piccadilly, London; royalacademy.org.uk

Great excitement among the crowds on Ladies Day at Royal Ascot

THE CONTEMPORARY CRAFT FESTIVAL

The craft first festival started in Bovey Tracey in 2003. Now hundreds of designer-maker stands, hand-picked for quality, are the heart of this annual prestigious and sophisticated three-day festival, while alongside are workshops and demonstrations, music and locally sourced food.
Bovey Tracey, Devon; craftfestival.co.uk

ROYAL ASCOT

It's about making a style statement as much as the horse racing. Much loved by Her Majesty the Queen, Royal Ascot attracts many of the world's finest horses, which compete for more than £8m in prize money, but it is also world-famous for its sartorial splendour and magnificent millinery. Don't miss the Royal Procession each day at 2 pm sharp: the Landau carriages, led by four Windsor greys, approach along the famous Straight Mile, signalling the start of the Royal Meeting.
Ascot, Berkshire; ascot.co.uk

A very familiar face at Wimbledon: Roger Federer

THE CHAMPIONSHIPS, WIMBLEDON

It began with 22 amateur tennis players who answered an ad in the leisure magazine *The Field* in June 1877. They each paid 11 shillings to take part in a lawn tennis meeting, with a final played in front of 200 people. These days, the attendance is more than 500,000, with a TV audience of millions around the globe and prize money totalling almost £40m. This year's tournament takes place from 28 June to 11 July. Now, where's that bowl of strawberries?

Wimbledon, London; wimbledon.com

WOOLFEST

Claiming to be the original British Wool Festival, Woolfest is a celebration of natural fibres – from fleece and livestock to spinning and yarn and then to finished craft – thus featuring more or less anything wool-related that you can think of, including a mass knit-in. This year it takes place on 25 and 26 June.

Cockermouth, Cumbria; woolfest.co.uk

THE ART AND ANTIQUES FAIR

The capital's longest-running – now in its 49th year – and most-respected vetted art and antiques fair is a highlight of London's summer calendar. It attracts fantastic dealers and enthusiasts from across the world looking for that inspirational, unique piece.

Olympia, London; olympia-art-antiques.com

WORLD CUSTARD PIE CHAMPIONSHIP

Back with a promise to be bigger, better and messier than ever, this hilarious family event draws teams from around the globe who, often in finest fancy-dress, fling pies at each other (the recipe is a closely guarded secret) across the village green. There are rules – a full pie in the face gets six points, for example – and a table of rankings. Will The Minions win again this year?

Coxheath, Kent; theworldcustardpie championship.co.uk

ISLE OF WIGHT FESTIVAL

The UK summer festival calendar kicks off in the Isle of Wight from 17 to 20 June with a diverse line-up that showcases new and emerging talent as well as legendary names in the music world. Organisers take pride in offering performances that you might not see elsewhere, as well as a uniquely relaxed atmosphere and friendly vibe.

Newport, Isle of Wight; isleofwightfestival.com

GOLOWAN

Cornish towns and villages once honoured midsummer with bonfires, flaming tar barrels and burning torches – until the late 19th century, when the perceived fire risk made insurance premiums too expensive. In 1991, however, the town of Penzance revived the tradition with a day of celebration. The event has now grown into a ten-day, community-led extravaganza with a serpent dance, Mock Mayor election, quayside fair, workshops, talks and a

TROOPING THE COLOUR

Trooping the Colour – a royal inspection of troops – has marked the official birthday of the British Sovereign for more than 260 years. The display of military precision, horsemanship and fanfare moves from Buckingham Palace to Horse Guards Parade, and concludes with an RAF fly-past and gun salute from Green Park.

Horse Guards Parade, Whitehall, London; qbp.army.mod.uk

The Welsh Guards march to Horseguards Parade during Trooping The Colour

SUMMER SOLSTICE

The summer solstice is one of the rare occasions when members of the public are allowed to enter the stone circle at Stonehenge. The sarsen stones, erected in the centre of the site in about 2,500 BC, were carefully positioned to line up with the movements of the sun, and at sunrise on 21 June its first rays shine from behind the Heel Stone, the ancient entrance to the stone circle, and into the heart of the prehistoric world heritage site. Thousands of people gather from all over the world to witness the spectacle, and English Heritage provides free managed open access to the site for individuals and groups conducting their own forms of ceremony and celebration. No alcohol is allowed at this peaceful, positive event – but if you wish to bring ceremonial mead you should contact customer services.

Stonehenge, Wiltshire; english-heritage.org.uk

An atmospheric experience is on offer at Stonehenge

THE GREAT KNARESBOROUGH BED RACE

About 90 teams race to raise money for local charities along a gruelling 2.4-mile course that includes steep slopes, cobbles and an icy swim at the end. The twist? They're all pushing a wheeled "bed" and a passenger. As well as the time trial there's also a splendid fancy-dress procession, with prizes for the best-dressed teams.

Knaresborough, North Yorkshire; bedrace.co.uk

Gearing up for The Bed Race

fireworks display. On Mazey Day, the final Saturday, a series of colourful parades – featuring awe-inspiring giant sculptures, singing, dancing, bands and performers – are watched by tens of thousands of locals and visitors, and the whole town becomes a huge market place for the day, with traders selling all manner of goods as well as food from around the world.

Penzance, Cornwall; golowanfestival.org

WYBUNBURY FIG PIE WAKES

If you wanted a definition of a quirky tradition, this is probably it. Every year, on a Saturday in June, the local community bakes fig pies and competes to roll them down the hill outside the Swan Inn. Apparently it all dates back to at least the early 1800s, though there was a break in the 20th century due to "unruly brawling". Revived in 1995 to raise money for the village's leaning church tower, it's now a charming and popular event, with stalls, refreshments, live music and other entertainment.

Wybunbury, Cheshire; facebook.com/wybunburyfigpie/

MIDSUMMER WATCH PARADE

A major midsummer spectacle, and one of the oldest festivals in Britain, Chester's colourful parade was first held in 1498. While many Tudor pageants featured "giants" – enormous structures made of buckram and pasteboard and carried by two or more men – Chester was unique in parading a whole family of giants comprising a mother, father and two daughters. They were accompanied by other huge, fantastic beasts and enormous moving floats called the "Mounts", as well as hobby horses, musicians, guildsmen, fools and children in the costumes of angels, goblins and green men. Announced by a loudly beating drum, it must have been the most exciting event of the year. However, Puritanism triumphed over pageantry in the 1660s, and the parade lapsed until the late 20th century, when it was revived with a single giant in 1989.

The parade has since grown bigger and bigger every year: these days schools and youth groups spend weeks creating characters, and it is once again a highlight of the Cheshire calendar. Setting off from Chester Town Hall Square, the route takes in much of the city centre.

Chester, Cheshire. midsummerwatch.co.uk

Images: Getty, Shutterstock, Alamy

BEAUTIFUL TOWN

POLPERRO

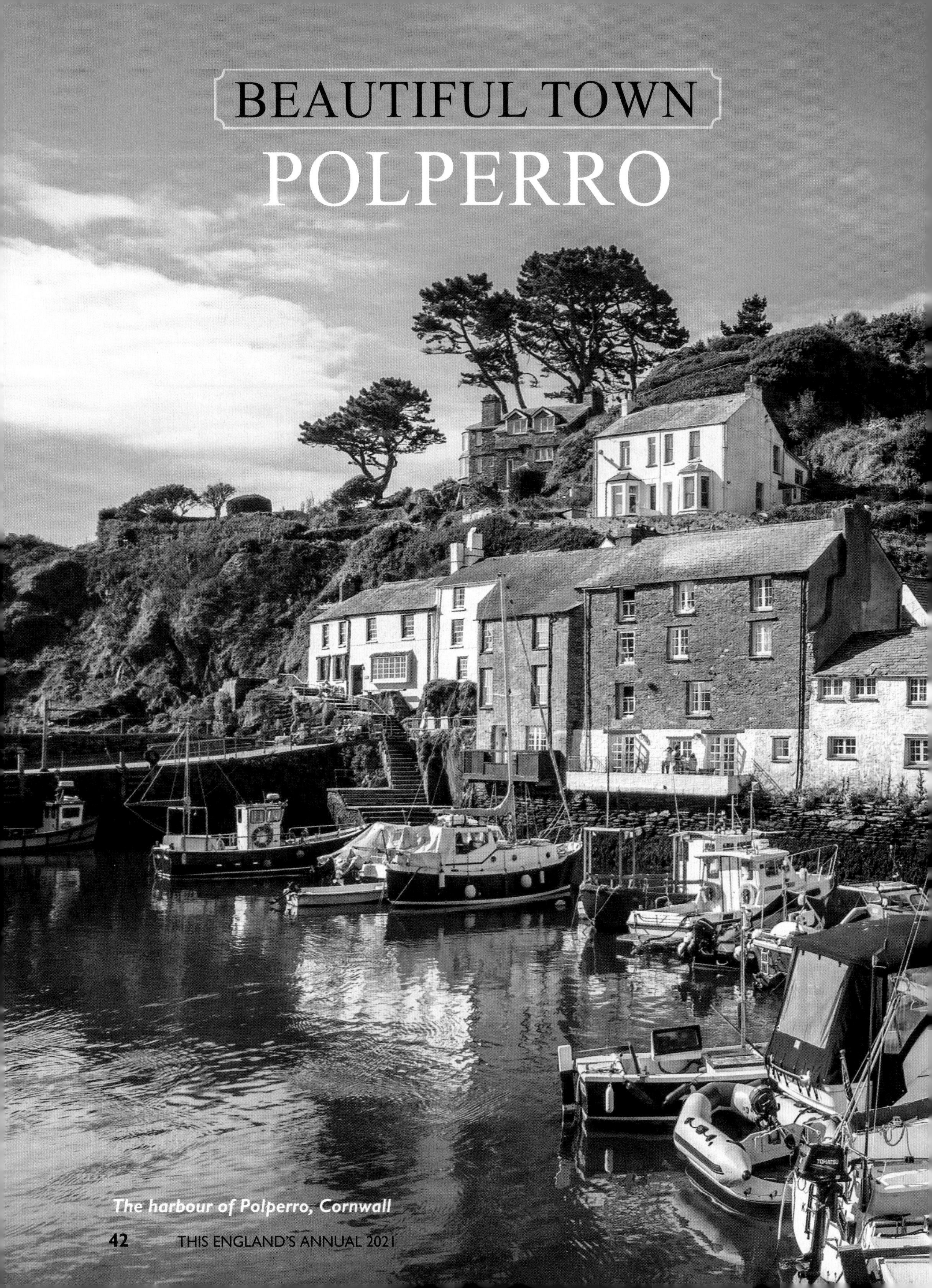

The harbour of Polperro, Cornwall

Relaxing at the Crumplehorn Inn and Mill

The 18th-century Three Pilchards pub

Morning light over Polperro Harbour

THE Cornish south coast is peppered with picturesque fishing villages and towns but none are as beautiful, or celebrated, perhaps, as Polperro. Located just south of Looe and 20 miles or so west of Plymouth, the eponymous village lies at the heart of the Polperro Heritage Coast, a wild and rocky stretch and an Area of Outstanding Natural Beauty.

Although a tourist honeypot, with an abundance of gift shops along the main high street known as The Coombe, Polperro retains an old-Cornish feel with its winding streets, too narrow for cars, and pretty cottages which cling to the cliffs that surround the harbour. Colourful boats bob in the turquoise waters and just beyond the harbour wall there's a little sandy beach that spreads out in front of Willy Wilcox cave which is uncovered at low tide. Willy Wilcox, an 18th-century smuggler, is said to haunt this spot after apparently drowning in the cave hiding from Customs officers.

Polperro has a long history of smuggling which belies its quiet appearance. Vast quantities of contraband was landed here during the latter half of the 18th century and taken by the wagonload over Bodmin Moor en route to London.

A visit to the Polperro Heritage Museum of Smuggling and Fishing, housed in an old pilchard factory, brings this to life. Here, amongst the drift nets and barrels, you'll find many treasures such as a cutlass which belonged to Robert Mark, a crewman of the infamous smuggling ship The Lottery.

The museum also tells the story of Polperro's significant fishing industry – it was famous for pilchards in the 19th century – and shows works by the distinguished artists and photographers who have been drawn to Polperro over the years. These include photographs taken by Lewis Harding and drawings by eminent naturalist Dr Jonathan Couch.

Still a working fishing port, Polperro's artistic tradition continues, too, with the Polperro Arts Foundation, a gallery overlooking the harbour and sandwiched between two popular pubs, The Three Pilchards and The Blue Peter. Founded by a group of local artists in 2001, as one of Polperro's few large spaces it hosts art workshops and events as well as regular exhibitions.

There are many pubs to tempt you. At the entrance to Polperro stands The Crumplehorn Inn & Mill which is said to take its unusual name from the curly-horned sheep or cows that once grazed the surrounding hillsides.

Dating to the 15th century, it was used as a counting house during Elizabethan times, when ships' captains could plunder foreign ships legally and split the proceeds with the crown. Each of the original blue slate flagstones in the upper bar has a lifting hole so any coins which dropped between the joints could be retrieved.

Grade II listed, The Three Pilchards is also a firm favourite, dating to the mid-1700s, as is The Blue Peter. Known affectionately as "The Blue", it offers a brilliant selection of local real ales to enjoy as the sun shimmers over the sea.

ISOBEL KING

DON'T MISS

A boat trip

The best way to see this beautiful stretch of Cornwall's coastline and appreciate Polperro's setting is a boat trip. Half-hour trips leave the harbour regularly during the high season and you might be lucky enough to see dolphins, basking sharks and sunfish, too. **Departing from the harbour quay by the beach. For further details visit: lovepolperro.com/what-to-do/boat-trips**

Shell House

Adorned with shells from around the world, this Grade II listed property is one of the most photographed and famous houses in Polperro. It was decorated by a retired naval man, Samuel Puckey, who started work in 1937 using his collection of shells gathered while in service. The work took five years to complete. Today, the house is let as a holiday home where lucky visitors can enjoy stunning harbour views. **The Warren, Polperro; 01503 272 320. To book, visit holidaycottagespolperro.co.uk**

Polperro Fisherman's Choir

Famous in Cornwall, this band of men was born out of a desire to preserve the tradition of the singing fisherman of Polperro. Their performances on the fish quay on selected Wednesday evenings in summer, have been described as one of Cornwall's ten best "free secrets". **polperrofishermenschoir.co.uk**

Images: Alamy, Shutterstock, Baz Richardson

Above: Ponies line up for judging during the Three Counties Show with the Malvern Hills in the background
Below: Cattle being led into the ring for judging at the Bath and West and Southern Counties Society Show at Oxford in 1934

Cattle are led as they are judged at the Devon County Show, which is one of the first shows in the county show season

IT'S SHOWTIME

Clare Gogerty explains why these centuries-old agricultural events are still such a hit today

Devon and Cornwall Longwool sheep are led out on to a field during the Royal Cornwall Show

Admiring the vintage tractors at the annual Bath And West Show, one of the oldest agricultural shows in England

THE summer months are prime county-show time. For the non-farming community, the local show is the place to head to see livestock in their buffed and clipped prime, to marvel at outrageous fruit and veg and to mosey among agricultural machinery, wondering what it does, before hitting the trade stands and buying a trug.

For farmers and landowners, however, a county show is a more serious business, offering a rare chance to get together with other breeders and competitors, parade their finest animals and learn about the latest developments in farming.

A celebration of rural life, a county show is the best way to understand the character of the locality in which it is situated. Animal breeds peculiar to the region are led before white-coated judges – often competitors in other categories themselves – looking for good conformation and fluid movement. Local produce is championed: cheese and cider at The Royal Bath and West Show; soft fruit at Kent County Show; cream and pasties at the Royal Cornwall. A county show is a distillation of the countryside that surrounds it.

"If you go to a festival you don't know what county you're in," Alan Lyons, Head of Shows at the Royal Bath and West Show says, "but in a county agricultural show, you know you are in a certain one because it celebrates the heritage, culture, food and drink of that county."

According to the Association of Show and Agricultural Organisations, six million of us visit such shows every year in the UK. This ever-expanding number could be because there is more to see and do than purely agricultural pursuits. Steam fairs, motorcycle stunt displays, flower shows and live music sit alongside tents filled with prize-winning poultry and show rings resounding with announcements about equine events.

Their growing popularity could also be because there is a renewed curiosity about the countryside from those who do not live in it.

"The average member of public has lost touch with how food is produced, how farming works and how rural life runs," Christopher Riddle, secretary of The Royal Cornwall Show, says. "Visiting a county show is an opportunity to find out; to see something that is invisible the rest of the time."

These days we take the permanent showgrounds with their multitude of trade stands, carefully managed competitions, attractions and parking for granted, but things weren't always thus. The earliest shows began as ploughing matches outside pubs, with prizes for categories such as fat sheep, turnip growing, farm carts and cheese making. Shows gradually grew in size with more categories added and, rather than remaining in one place, began to tour the country.

"The original concept of the Royal Bath and West Show was to educate farmers and landowners about how to feed a growing population," Alan Lyons explains. "The best way to do this was to tour a show with exhibitions of latest crop cultivations and previews of livestock. The Bath and West Show moved all over the country, from as far north as Nottingham down to Penzance and across to Cardiff."

The arrival of a county show to a town was a big event, with pedigree animals arriving by train or, in one case, travelling from Barnstaple to Cardiff by steam ferry. Moving livestock around the country was a logistical nightmare and an event in itself.

"It was a staggering thing to manage. When a train pulled into St Albans, the animals being unloaded and led to the show fields became the spectacle. People saw things they wouldn't have access to normally, including, on occasion, prize-winning animals belonging to the Royal family."

These travelling shows were also a gathering place for farmers to inspect, and buy, livestock.

"This was before the internet or mass media: if you wanted to advertise your livestock you had to take it to a show."

Restricted movement before widespread car-ownership or frequent rail services meant that the arrival of the travelling show was an important social date for the farming community.

"County shows have always been a great meeting place," Christopher Riddle says. "Going back 100 to 200 years, farming folk didn't get together very often; the shows provided that opportunity. Today, getting together at a show remains important socially and for mental health. Farms don't have as many staff as they used to, and farming can be a lonely life."

Alan Lyons agrees.

"Closure of smaller livestock markets, fewer people working on farms and delivery of animal feed means farmers are increasingly isolated. Walk down an avenue of any county show and you will see friends meeting up: it's the one time of year they get together. The shows are important social occasions for the wellbeing of the rural community."

>

A steam engine attracts a lot of interest on the opening day of the Royal Cornwall Show

Above: Texel sheep are judged during the first day of the Great Yorkshire Show outside Harrogate
Below: The Band of the Royal Armoured Corps in the main arena at the Great Yorkshire Show

HRH Prince of Wales admires the prize-winning cattle at the Great Yorkshire Show

SIX OF THE BEST COUNTY SHOWS, 2021

1. Royal Cornwall Show, Wadebridge, Cornwall, 10-12 June 2021
Farmers have brought sheep, cattle and horses to the Royal Cornwall for over 200 years and there are hundreds of classes to admire. Head to the main ring for the grand parade of prize-winning animals to see livestock in peak condition. Alongside the agricultural attractions, including sheep-shearing competitions and sheepdog trials, Cornish-grown and produced food is showcased. There is a steam fair, live music and around 1,000 trade stands. Run by Royal Cornwall Agricultural Association, the show covers 95 acres and is held on its permanent showground near Wadebridge.
royalcornwallshow.org

2. Royal Three Counties Show, Malvern, Worcestershire, 18-20 June 2021
Founded in 1794 for farm workers in Herefordshire, the show expanded to include Worcestershire and Gloucestershire in 1798, rotating between the three counties. With a permanent showground since 1958, the show is still strong on agriculture with 900 classes of competitions. Its Farming Village is the place to go to see livestock and chat to farmers, and talks on food and farming are held in the Wellington Boot Theatre. There is also blacksmithing to admire and the rare opportunity to see men competitively climbing poles in the forestry area.
threecounties.co.uk

3. Royal Bath and West, Shepton Mallet, Somerset, 28-30 May 2021
England's biggest county show was planned to run over three days

Shows stopped touring as counties established their own agricultural societies and, from the 1800s, ran their own shows or combined with other counties like the Three Counties Show and the Bath and West Show.

"Around 1870, the shows' content began to change to cater for increasing numbers of non-farming visitors. Trade stands that weren't necessarily agricultural were introduced. Old photographs show fantastic haberdashery stands, pots and pans and general things for sale. A tailor would tour shows, making up suits."

A formal dress code was important then and still operates at some shows: on the first day of the Royal Cornwall, Alan Lyons advises you definitely need to wear a jacket and tie; on the second maybe lose the tie; by the third you might just get away with jeans and deck shoes. Certain shows, especially in the Eastern counties like the Royal Norfolk, are still very smart; others, like the Three Counties, are more relaxed.

For those who aren't farmers but who love the rural lifestyle, a county show is a chance to go foot to hoof with a variety of animals and with those who raise them. If expert knowledge of animal husbandry is what you are after, a county show is the place to go.

"It's startling how people don't have the opportunity to have close contact with animals," Christopher Riddle says. "Many dream of buying a house with a little piece of land to keep a few sheep or chickens. A county show is a good place to find out about the reality behind that dream."

Experts like Doreen Smillie-Grey who, with husband Steve, competes and judges in many county shows and whose

(rather than four) for the first time in 2020. This does not diminish its scale: livestock is still at its heart (try to catch the Grand Parade of prize-winning animals), but there is more of a festival atmosphere these days, with live music in the Pilton Tent (sponsored by Glastonbury Festival), daredevil motorcycling and a 7¼ inch railway to take you around the site, among other attractions. Fittingly, for a show in the heart of the West Country, it also hosts the British Cider Championships and British Cheese Awards.
bathandwest.com

A rider competes in a show jumping event at the Great Yorkshire Show

4. Great Yorkshire Show, Harrogate, Yorkshire, 13-15 July 2021
Originally a peripatetic show, the Great Yorkshire has been on a permanent 100-acre site in Harrogate since 1950. It is one of the biggest agricultural shows with 8,500 animals in competition for prizes, including many different breeds of Yorkshire sheep. Top-level show jumping takes place in the main ring with the prestigious Cock o' the North trophy up for grabs. There is also live music, a fashion show, falconry, cookery demonstrations, a food hall showcasing Yorkshire produce, and motorcycle formation teams.
greatyorkshireshow.co.uk

5. Lambeth Country Show, Brockwell Park, London, 17-18 July 2021
A victim of its own success, this free urban country show, which has run since 1974, has erected a fence and banned the bringing in of alcohol to control the crowds. A country-comes-to-town theme is still central with its legendary carved vegetable competition, sheep shearing, owl displays and craft and food stalls, but music plays an increasing part. Its Village Green and Main Stage attract well-known bands and give the show the feel of a summer festival in a park.
lambethcountryshow.co.uk

6. Kent County Show, Maidstone, Kent, Date to be confirmed
Coinciding with the fruit harvest, the Kent County Show shows off the Garden of England's bounty of strawberries, cherries et al with the National Cherry and Soft Fruit Show held here every year. There are also three days of livestock competitions, wool and honey tents, and a woodland area with working horses dragging timber along the forest floor. Expect to see a working dairy, Morris dancing and even camel racing, too.
kentshowground.co.uk

smallholding is wreathed in rosettes for her prize-winning Rylance sheep, are on hand to point them in the right direction.

"At a county show, people are educated without realising it," she says, "particularly about where their food comes from. For us a show is foremost a showcase for our flock and is extremely competitive, but we are also happy to spread the word about raising and caring for animals."

This interest in where food comes from chimes with the latest development in county shows: a growth of interest in locally produced food and drink.

"Shows have been very quick to pick up the challenge," Alan Lyons says. "Most have educational features on how to milk a cow, identifying different crops, explaining machinery."

They are a showcase for British food and drink generally, with food halls and cookery demonstrations providing an outlet for producers and a tasting smorgasbord for visitors.

County shows have come a long way. To survive, they evolved to encompass activities with a more general appeal. Although livestock and agriculture remain at their heart, these days you are as likely to test drive an electric car or sample a vegan brownie as marvel at prize-winning bulls led around the main ring by their owners.

Alan Lyons says, "County shows are not museums, they will always be relevant. They are living, vibrant events that have something for everyone."

For more information: Association of Show and Agricultural Organisations (asao.co.uk)

Images: Getty

The red squirrel's numbers have declined due to?

The grass snake is one of how many species of reptiles in the UK?

FLORA AND FAUNA QUIZ

Test your wildlife knowledge with our brain-teasing questions

1. The ball-shaped growths on the leaves of oak trees made by the gall wasp, called oak galls or oak apples, were used to make what essential product for writers until the 19th century?

2. The ash was the tree of which Greek god in ancient mythology?

3. Which county is home to the National Trust's oldest tree, a 2,500-year-old yew called the Ankerwycke Yew, under which King Henry VIII is said to have courted Anne Boleyn?

4. Which county is home to the largest vegetated shingle spit in Europe?

5. What British mammal is responsible for creating holts (underground dens), couches (above-ground resting sites), spraints (dung) and slides (for entering water)?

6. What is the name of the disease carried by the grey squirrel, *Sciurus carolinensis*, that is often fatal to the indigenous red squirrel, *Sciurus vulgaris*?

7. Which of the UK's native mustelids are the only examples to have semi-retractable claws?

8. The berries, leaves and bark from which native tree were traditionally used in the production of colourfully patterned Harris tweed?

9. Name the author of some of the country's best-loved children's stories about wildlife. She lived in the lake district and left most of her estate to the National Trust.

10. How many species of reptiles are there in Great Britain?

11. Which poet wrote, "Wind warns November's done with. The blown leaves make bat-shapes, web-winged and furious"?

12. Who wrote the following about the unique sounds of native British trees: "The holly whistles as it battles with itself; the ash hisses amid its quaverings; the beech rustles while its flat boughs rise and fall" in *Under the Greenwood Tree*?

13. Which female beetle makes an attractive display every summer

Ted Hughes's poem is about which freshwater fish?

Images: Shutterstock

It was used for weaving; what is the name of this grass?

It was tree of the year in 2014, but where is it and what's it called?

with bioluminescence?

14. The natural bacteriostatic properties of which plant's flowering stalks have been used for centuries in a thirst-quenching national activity?

15. A ubiquitous 19th-century oil painting of Great Britain's largest mammal, The Monarch of the Glen by Sir Edwin Landseer, was commissioned to hang in which palace?

16. Which medieval recluse lived on one of the group of islands which are now home to over 100,000 sea birds, including the locally named "Cuddy's"?

17. Which common plant found throughout the British Isles is thought to cure warts, can be used in a salad, for making wine and coffee and as a diuretic?

18. What is the evil-sounding common name of the marshland pinky-purple flower that was traditionally used for treating skin conditions such as scabies?

19. Which tiny moth's only known breeding colony in the UK is within the perimeter fencing of Dungeness A and B nuclear power stations in Kent?

20. Which freshwater fish – "Killers from the egg: the malevolent aged grin" – features in an eponymous poem by former Poet Laureate Ted Hughes?

21. Which common coastal weed is used by the beauty industry to turn back time and is widely used in skin-care products such as anti-ageing creams?

Which football team has taken its nickname from the thrush?

22. At around 8,000 hectares, what is the UK's largest nature reserve on the east coast of England and stretching over two counties?

23. What was the name of the banker and naturalist who, in May 1912, was the catalyst for a new organisation to protect the British Isles' best places for wildlife?

24. What is a broad-bodied chaser?

25. What is the name of grass that was once used in weaving and today plays a vital role in stabilising coastal sand dunes?

26. Which now common British breeding bird was only first seen in Britain in 1952 and first bred in 1955 in a Norfolk garden?

27. Robin Hood was said to hide in this tree, winner of the Woodland Trust's Tree of the Year in 2014. What is its name and where is it?

28. What football team has the nickname the Throstles? The name was chosen in the late 19th century because the team used to change in a local public house which kept a pet thrush (or throstle) in a cage.

29. In which year was the inaugural exhibition of the Society of Wildlife Artists (SWLA) held in London?

30. What creature is portrayed in John Clare's 19th-century poem "kicked and torn and beaten out he lies And leaves his hold and cackles, groans, and dies"?

To see how you got on, turn to page 106 for answers.

View of the Big Dipper, 1923

A RIDE THROUGH NOSTALGIA

As Blackpool Pleasure Beach celebrates its 125th anniversary, Barry McCann looks back on the rollercoaster history of this Lancashire landmark

THEME parks are generally thought of as a post-war import from America, but there is at least one in this country that not only dates back to the Victorian era but also remains an iconic part of English seaside heritage – Blackpool Pleasure Beach. The 42-acre amusement park, which incorporates two luxury hotels, purpose-built ice arena and numerous theatres, has been owned and run by the same family for four generations, and was founded in 1896.

Looking at the park today, it is perhaps hard to believe that this tangle of sinuous metal rollercoaster tracks is really that old. Rides use the latest amusement-park technology, reaching to the sky, and the place pulsates with the energy of delighted thrill seekers. With millions of visitors a year, Blackpool Pleasure Beach is undoubtedly a success story. Unlike many attractions, it has managed to thrive and adapt through changing times.

Its origins, however, are humble. The story begins with business partners William George Bean and John Outhwaite. Whilst working in the amusement machine industry in Philadelphia, London-born Bean was inspired by the rides he experienced on Coney Island, New York, and realised that something similar could work in England. Blackpool was a fitting location. The city had grown rapidly on the back of the industrial revolution and the development of the railway made it an easy destination for industrial northern workers during their annual holidays.

On the South Shore a small fairground, with a few roundabouts, switchback railway, games stalls and fortune tellers, already existed. Here the duo's first ride was built: the Hotchkiss Bicycle Railroad.

"We wanted to found an American-style amusement park, the fundamental principal of which is to make adults feel like children again and to inspire a gaiety of a primarily innocent character," Bean declared at the ride's opening. Over the next decade, a playground was exactly what Bean and Outhwaite created. Additional rides joined the Bicycle Railway:

Images: Blackpool Pleasure Beach

in 1904 a rotary swing, the Captive Flying Machines, designed by prolific inventor Sir Hiram Maxim (now chiefly remembered for his weaponry inventions), and in 1905 a water-chute ride, River Caves of the World. The Velvet Coaster, so called for its velvet seats, was installed. The Scenic Railway became a reality in 1907.

In 1911 the House of Nonsense opened, where for 3d adventurous punters contended with shaking floors, a joy wheel that spun them outwards and a hall of mirrors. Sadly, that same year saw the death of John Outhwaite, who left most of the remaining business to Bean with a minority stake given to the rest to his family.

Bean still had more contributions to make to the park before his own death in 1929, and the Pleasure Beach expanded further into its present 42-acre site. Although development was curtailed by World War I, the 1920s saw an Indian-Palace-style casino built, housing a billiard hall, cinema, restaurant and gift shop. The famous Big Dipper, which still delights visitors today, was also installed with a boating pool.

The park was inherited by Bean's only daughter, Lillian-Doris, who had married Oxford Natural Sciences graduate Leonard Thompson the year before. Thompson agreed to take over the running of the Pleasure Beach and when the Outhwaites sold their share to the Thompsons, Leonard was given complete ownership of the operation.

Challenges lay ahead. The Pleasure Beach had lost both its original founders just before the onset of the Depression and this period was, of course, followed by World War II. People continued to flock to Blackpool, however, and to the Pleasure Beach in particular, to escape life's grim reality – if only for a short while.

Leonard met this demand with continuing reconstruction. The Velvet Coaster was replaced in 1933 by the Rollercoaster, designed by the celebrated Charles Paige. Two years later, Paige went one better with the Grand National, consisting of twin rollercoasters following a parallel circuit, their riders vying to be the one that finishes first. The casino was rebuilt in a modern art-deco style by award-winning architect Joseph Emberton, who also designed a 2,000 seater Ice Dome which doubled as a venue for ice-skating shows and a rink for the public to try the sport.

The rides roll on into the evening

Current Managing Director Amanda Thompson maintains it was this constant development and improvement which led to Blackpool Pleasure Beach's continuing success.

"It's constantly evolving. It has always been a leader in terms of amusement-park trends and ride advancement and this has allowed us to endure for so long."

The park even stayed open

>

> during World War II thanks in part to an additional population of evacuees, mainly children and civil servants, in Blackpool. An RAF station opened in the town to train recruits and the resort also became a popular destination for service personnel on rest and recuperation. This meant their families would be visiting the town, and not just during the summer holidays, so the park stayed open as an all-year attraction to help boost morale.

The 1950s saw a new threat: the rise of cheaper foreign package holidays. Canny Leonard responded with investment on a grand scale and the creation of ever more ambitious concepts to continue to satisfy the crowds. A new cable-car ride crossed the park and the celebrated Alice in Wonderland ride was installed – Amanda's favourite ride for its "pure escapism". The Log Flume built in 1967 was the only one constructed outside of the USA, and was the biggest in the world.

The Thompson family on The Big Dipper

After 47 years of running the business, Leonard died in 1976 and Doris took over as chairman. The post of Managing Director went to their only son, Geoffrey Thompson, who had already masterminded the opening of themed bars in the casino building, such as Diamond Lil's Saloon, with its Wild West décor, and the Edwardian bar steeped in period detail.

"People want more than just a place to have a drink nowadays; they like a little novelty attached to it!" Geoffrey said at the time. The success of the bars proved him right.

He went on to leave his own stamp on the park during the 1970s, buoyed by the opening of the M55 link to the Fylde coast. Blackpool was now easier and quicker to reach for day trippers looking for a fun day out.

Notable new rides during this period included the Revolution, the country's first rollercoaster with a 360 degree loop. However, Geoffrey's crowning achievements came in the 1990s, firstly with the opening of The Big One in 1994. With a drop of 235 feet, "it was the tallest and fastest rollercoaster in the world when it opened and it changed Blackpool's skyline for ever," says Amanda. Then in 2000 came Valhalla, a spectacular £15 million Viking-themed water ride. This ride guarantees passengers a bigger soaking than even the Log Flume ever did – hence the provision of body driers for those without waterproofs!

Geoffrey, who made many visionary additions to the park, sadly died of a heart attack in June 2004. Doris Thompson passed away nine days later, on the day of her son's funeral. Responsibility passed to Amanda, Geoffrey's

FAMOUS FACES

There have been a number of illustrious visitors to Blackpool Pleasure Beach over its long history. Gracie Fields arrived in 1934 to film scenes for *Sing as We Go*. In this musical comedy she played Gracie Platt, who finds herself out of work with the closure of her local mill and comes to Blackpool seeking employment. Finding it at the Pleasure Beach, she works in side shows such as The Human Spider and The Vanishing Girl.

Perhaps even stranger than fiction, that same year saw a visit by Marlene Dietrich who decided to give the Big Dipper a try. Unfortunately she lost an earring during the ride which fell into the boating pool below. It turned up 73 years later when the pool was drained to make way for a new ride!

After the war, Walt Disney visited and gave permission to use *Alice in Wonderland* for the Pleasure Beach ride.

"My father worked very closely with and gave lots of advice to Walt Disney when he was planning his amusement parks," says Amanda. "The global attractions industry is very special – we all work very closely, and I'm sure that Blackpool Pleasure Beach has inspired generations of industry professionals to develop, operate and design amusement parks around the world today."

Icon is the UK's first double-launch rollercoaster

The Captive Flying Machines and Scenic Railway, 1907

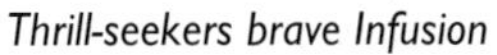

Thrill-seekers brave Infusion

Managing Director Amanda Thompson

The park is a tangle of sinuous metal rollercoaster tracks

PLEASURE BEACH IN NUMBERS

-1: the G-force as you free-fall on Ice Blast which causes a feeling of weightlessness

£16.25 million: invested in Icon, the UK's first double-launch rollercoaster

65 degree drop: making The Big One rollercoaster the steepest in the world

80 feet high: Valhalla is the world's biggest indoor dark ride

1930: constructed in this year, the Ghost Train is the earliest example of a ride of this kind

2,600 tonnes: the amount of steel used to build The Big One – if laid end to end it would stretch for 40 miles

15,000: nuts and bolts used every year

500,000: candyflosses sold every season – enough to returf Wembley Stadium four times over!

eldest daughter who, having been a director for over 15 years, during which she staged lavish shows at the park's Globe Theatre, was not without experience.

"I find it very rewarding to be able to continue my family's legacy by leading such an iconic amusement park. I also love that I get to work in such an amazing industry."

Amanda received an OBE in 2012 for services to tourism. She takes particular pride in being Chairman of the IAAPA, the global association for the attractions industry, as her father and grandfather held this position.

Amanda's management has seen the park brought truly into the 21st century. The introduction of a basic admission charge several years back may not have been popular at the time, but has paid dividends, with a cleaner, more spacious and secure site for visitors to enjoy.

Her programme of upgrades also saw old favourites retired to make room for new ones. In 2005 the Log Flume was replaced by Infusion, the park's first new rollercoaster since The Big One opened 13 years previously. It was joined by Icon in 2018.

While continually introducing new and challenging rides, much of Pleasure Beach's heritage is still evident. The casino building, having been refurbished over the years, is in use. Sir Hiram Maxim's unique Flying Machines ride thrills to this day, as does the River Caves ride. Classic rollercoasters the Big Dipper and the Grand National still attract enthusiasts from all over.

"I think the original founders would like what they see," Amanda says. "There are still elements that are the same as when my great-grandfather, W.G. Bean, established the park in 1896. I think he would enjoy seeing all the new innovations, but also be delighted that some of the original rides are still here."

Is it just for thrill seekers?

"Truthfully I believe there is something for everyone at Blackpool Pleasure Beach," Amanda replies. "If you like thrilling rides, we have ten rollercoasters – if you prefer gentle rides we have the Pleasure Beach Express and River Caves, to name just two. We have Nickelodeon Land, and Wallace and Gromit's Thrill-O-Matic for our younger visitors, and if you don't like rides at all we have amazing live entertainment, such as the stunning Hot Ice show."

Still true to its founding principles, I can't help but feel that while there are the young and the young at heart, Blackpool Pleasure Beach will remain a jewel in the English seaside crown.

"I hope that when people visit us they take away some wonderful memories of their time spent here," says Amanda. "I like to think that there is a little piece of Blackpool in everyone".

A year-long series of events will be announced to mark 125 years of Blackpool Pleasure Beach.
525 Ocean Boulevard, Blackpool, FY4 1EZ. 0333 003 2212; blackpoolpleasurebeach.com

As Imperceptibly as Grief

By Emily Dickinson

As imperceptibly as Grief
The Summer lapsed away –
Too imperceptible at last
To seem like Perfidy –
A Quietness distilled
As Twilight long begun,
Or Nature spending with herself
Sequestered Afternoon –
The Dusk drew earlier in –
The Morning foreign shone –
A courteous, yet harrowing Grace,
As Guest, that would be gone –
And thus, without a Wing
Or service of a Keel
Our Summer made her light escape
Into the Beautiful.

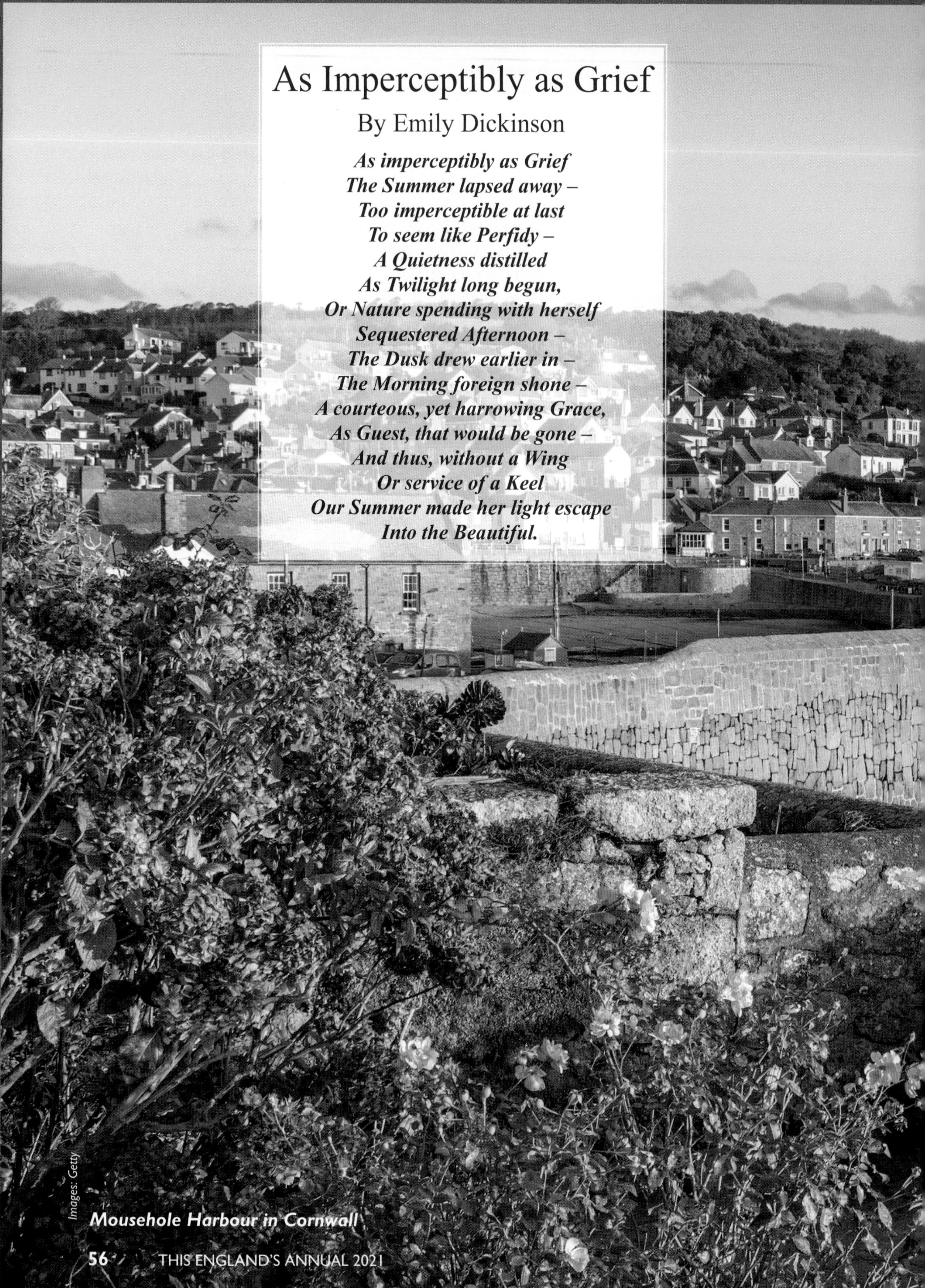

Mousehole Harbour in Cornwall

SUMMER TO AUTUMN

Events including the Bristol Balloon Fiesta and the Egton Bridge Gooseberry Show, plus discover the birds of Britain >

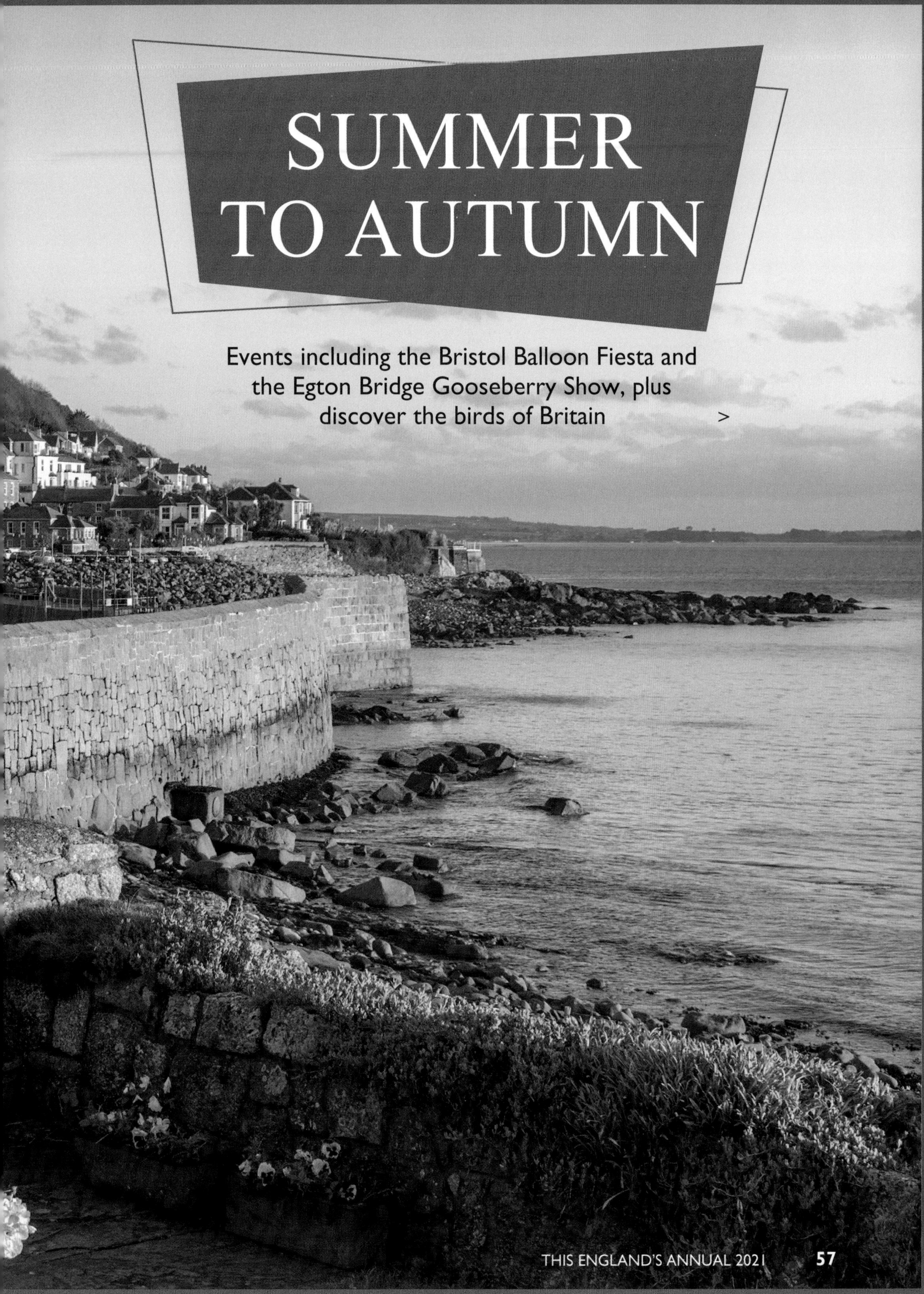

SUMMER TO AUTUMN

From racing snails to royal regattas, there's something for everyone at this time of year, Katherine Sorrell tells us

SWAN UPPING

Since before the 12th century, the reigning King or Queen has been entitled to claim ownership of any unmarked mute swans swimming in open water. Why? Because cygnets were a delicacy much prized for feasts and banquets. In modern times, the ceremony of "swan upping", the annual census of the swan population on the River Thames, has become an important element of wildlife conservation. In the third week of July a flotilla of traditional Thames rowing skiffs, manned by Swan Uppers in vivid scarlet rowing shirts and headed by The Queen's Swan Marker, spend five days rowing their way up the river in order to weigh and measure the cygnets and check them for any signs of injury.

River Thames, between Sunbury and Abingdon; royal.uk/swans

Swans are weighed and measured at Staines on the Thames

Snails racing in one of the knockout heats of the championships

WORLD SNAIL RACING CHAMPIONSHIPS

They say that Congham is to snail racing what Newmarket is to horse racing. The championships are part of Congham's annual fete, which raises money for the local church, and all newcomers are welcome. Simply select your garden snail – giant foreign ones are banned – and turn up. Ready, set . . . slow!

Congham, Norfolk; snailracing.net

The Proms start in July and finish in September in a blaze of flags

BBC PROMS

The biggest classical music festival in the world returns for its annual two-month run at the Royal Albert Hall. The aim is to bring the finest classical music to as many people as possible at affordable prices and in an informal atmosphere. The broad programme of music includes classical favourites, contemporary world premieres and family concerts.

Royal Albert Hall, London; bbc.co.uk/proms

Henley is famed for the Royal Regatta

HENLEY ROYAL REGATTA

It's both a sporting and social highlight set in picturesque Henley: an international rowing regatta with more than 300 races, from single sculls to eights. **Henley-on-Thames, Oxfordshire; hrr.co.uk**

HENLEY FESTIVAL

Henley takes centre stage again. Not your usual festival – the dress code is black tie, so get dressed up or you won't be allowed in. As well as visual arts, top-class comedy and troupes of roving entertainers, there's fine dining and spectacular firework displays, while the extensive programme of live music includes headliners James Blunt, Madness and Sophie Ellis-Bextor. It runs 7-11 July. **Henley-on-Thames, Oxfordshire; henley-festival.co.uk**

GARSTANG ICE CREAM FESTIVAL

Do you like sprinkles, a 99 or strawberry syrup? Gelato or sorbet? Cone or tub? This free festival of ice-cream, run on National Ice Cream Day (the third Sunday in July) has everything ice-cream related you can imagine, plus live entertainment and plenty of family fun. Garstang is the world's first Fairtrade Town, with a medieval centre and a weekly market that's been running since 1310. The town's traders launched the festival in 2018, bringing together local ice-cream makers and artisan ice-cream specialists. **Garstang, Lancashire; garstangicecreamfestival.co.uk**

NYETIMBER DORSET SEAFOOD FESTIVAL

Celebrating Dorset's links with the sea and its fishing communities, the UK's largest free seafood festival takes place around Weymouth's Old Harbour. Explore the journey from sea to plate in the Seafood Village, where you can try many different species of fish and shellfish from around 100 stalls, learn about sustainability and responsible fishing, watch demonstrations by local and national chefs, join in with hands-on sessions and listen to debates about the future of our seas. **Weymouth, Dorset; dorsetseafood.co.uk**

THE GAME FAIR

This festival of the countryside has been described as Glastonbury for the green wellie brigade, and has run since 1958. Expect air guns and archery, four by fours and fishing, gun dogs and gamekeeping as well as traditional crafts, shopping and a programme of displays and activities. The event alternates between the grand country houses of Ragley Hall in Warwickshire and Hatfield House in Hertfordshire, and this year takes place 23-25 July at Hatfield. **Hatfield House, Hertfordshire; thegamefair.org**

WHITSTABLE OYSTER FESTIVAL

The weekend of Whitstable's Oyster Festival celebrates an age-old tradition that dates back to the Norman times. Proceedings officially begin with the Landing of the Oysters, where a symbolic haul is landed on the beach, received by the Lord Mayor and blessed by the clergy. Then there's food, drink and live music galore, plus traditional events including an oyster parade, a "mud tug" and the building of "grotters" (small mounds of oyster shells lit by candles on the inside) on the beach at sunset. **Various locations, Whitstable, Kent; whitstableoysterfestival.co.uk**

Prince Charles and Camilla taste oysters

GREAT YORKSHIRE SHOW

This three-day show is one of the biggest agricultural events in the English calendar, showcasing the best of British farming, food and the countryside. In addition to the thousands of animals, from cattle to sheep, pigs to pigeons, which compete in the judging rings, there are demonstrations, displays, shopping and fashion shows. It all finishes with one of the most prestigious show-jumping classes in the country, the Cock o' the North. Read more about England's strong county show tradition on pages 44-49. **Great Yorkshire Showground, Harrogate, Yorkshire; greatyorkshireshow.co.uk**

>

SILVERSTONE CLASSIC

The world's biggest classic motor-racing festival features the cream of historic racing action, from Formula One and sports cars to GT and touring car grids. The Classic is also renowned for its RetroRun of classic (pre 2000) cars, superb displays by more than 100 different car clubs, unique car auctions and live music concerts staged at sunset on both Friday and Saturday evenings.

Silverstone Circuit, Northamptonshire; silverstoneclassic.com

Racing at Silverstone in earlier days

WINCHESTER HAT FAIR

Not a fair all about hats at all, but rather the UK's longest-running festival of street performance and outdoor arts, with street theatre, comedy and music. It's free, family friendly and takes place across the historic city of Winchester during the first weekend of July.

Winchester, Hampshire; hatfair.co.uk

See a selection of cheeses at the UK's biggest show

INTERNATIONAL CHEESE AND DAIRY AWARDS

It's the biggest cheese show in the world. Alongside more than 5,500 cheeses from countries around the globe, there are also accompaniments from port to pickle, celebrity chefs, a family kitchen and the ever-popular cheese-and-beer pavilion. Ah, but I do like a bit of gorgonzola.

Nantwich, Cheshire; internationalcheeseawards.co.uk

CHERTSEY BLACK CHERRY FAIR

Held every year on the second Saturday in July, Black Cherry Fair was first established in 1440. The lively community event features stalls, competitions, a music stage, live auction and fairground, plus a themed procession.

Chertsey, Surrey; blackcherryfair.com

BUXTON INTERNATIONAL FESTIVAL

The hills are alive with the sound of . . . opera! Buxton's annual festival runs for 17 days each July, presenting world-class opera alongside a renowned series of concerts with celebrated international performers, plus talks from some of the UK's best-known authors and speakers. One of Europe's most impressive (yet friendly) opera and culture festivals, it has been running for more than 40 years, and is the only one of its kind in the north of England. Dates for 2021 are 2-18 July.

Buxton, Derbyshire; buxtonfestival.co.uk

THE DRAGONFLY FESTIVAL, MANCHESTER

Celebrate National Dragonfly Week with this family-oriented festival. There will be stalls, arts and crafts, food and the chance to meet some dragons!

Prince's Park, Irlam, Manchester; lancswt.org.uk

RHS HAMPTON COURT PALACE GARDEN FESTIVAL

Summer colour, gardening inspiration and beautiful blooms set against the backdrop of one of the UK's most iconic palaces. Explore the show gardens, admire the plants, shop for your outside space, have a picnic by Long Water or catch an expert talk to fill you with gardening inspiration.

Hampton Court Palace, East Molesey, Surrey; rhs.org.uk

Explore the beautiful show gardens at the Hampton Court Festival

AUGUST 2021

GILBERT AND SULLIVAN FESTIVAL

This celebration of the works of the Victorian operatic duo, the country's most successful and enduring musical partnership, brings together a mix of professional and leading amateur groups who stage 40 full-scale performances.

Royal Hall, Harrogate, North Yorkshire; gsfestivals.org

KYNREN: AN EPIC TALE OF ENGLAND

Held in Bishop Auckland every Saturday in summer, this multi-award-winning open-air performance employs a cast of 1,500 to reveal the history, myth and legend of England over 2,000 years. Expect invasions, wars, daily life and change as actors bring to life Boudicca's doomed uprising against the Romans, the clash of Viking and Anglo-Saxon leaders, King Arthur's encounter with the Lady of the Lake, King Charles's final journey to the executioner's block, Queen Victoria's Diamond Jubilee and the bravery of soldiers on the battlefields. This live-action show takes place in the evening and features original music and choreography mingled with stunts, shows of horsemanship, special effects and pyrotechnics.

Flatts Farm, Bishop Auckland, County Durham; kynren.com

A spectacular show on English history

The yachts race in front of Queen Victoria's former home, Osborne House

COWES WEEK

The oldest and largest annual sailing regatta in the world is now a key feature in the British sporting calendar. It stages up to 40 daily races for around a thousand boats, and offers a mix of competitive sailing and social activities. The famous fireworks take place on the final Friday of the event.

Cowes, Isle of Wight; cowesweek.co.uk

LYTHAM 1940S WARTIME WEEKEND

Lytham's popular event attracts visitors from all over the country and this year will take place on 14 and 15 August. Roll back the decades and immerse yourself in the spirit of the wartime era with singing, dancing, big bands, educational talks, battle re-enactments, historic vehicles and vintage traders. Daytime entertainment in the main marquee is free.

Lytham Green, Lytham St Annes, Lancashire; discoverfylde.co.uk/lytham1940s

BOURNEMOUTH AIR FESTIVAL

There are four days of action and entertainment in the air, on land and at sea in the UK's biggest festival of aviation. As well as flying displays throughout the afternoon and early evening from the world's most powerful and agile aircraft, there are exciting performances, military displays and demonstrations, live music, street entertainment and even pyrotechnic night flying.

Bournemouth seafront, between the Boscombe and Bournemouth piers; bournemouthair.co.uk

CASTLE HOWARD PROMS

A memorable evening set against the glorious backdrop of one of England's finest historic houses. One of the largest UK proms concerts outside Hyde Park, it includes popular classics, songs from musicals and all your flag-waving favourites from the Proms. Proceedings are topped off by a Spitfire flyover and spectacular firework finale.

Castle Howard Estate, York; castlehoward.co.uk

BBC COUNTRYFILE LIVE

Join the TV show's presenters for four days of rural-related entertainment – from talks on climate, farming and wildlife to pig agility and sheepdog trials.

Windsor Great Park, Berkshire; countryfilelive.com

The BBC Countryfile presenters

>

> ## GREAT BRITISH BEER FESTIVAL

It's organiser CAMRA's 50th anniversary this year, and Britain's biggest beer festival is sure to be better than ever. Experience the natural magic of grain to glass, while enjoying live music and fabulous food – this is the biggest pub in the world, after all. Tutored tastings and other educational experiences are also scheduled, ensuring that attendees get the most out of the festival's choice of more than a thousand real ales, ciders, perries and international beers.

Olympia, London; gbbf.org.uk

CHILLI FIESTA

This family-friendly festival offers a wide range of activities, all linked to chillies. Find out how to use the hot stuff in your cooking with talks and demonstrations, dance to live Latin music, learn about gardening or explore herb-inspired cocktail making. There are also children's activities, produce stalls and a firework finale, plus a distinctive feel-good factor overall.

West Dean College, Chichester, West Sussex; westdean.org.uk.

NOTTING HILL CARNIVAL

This joyful, diverse and vibrant community-led event has been taking over the streets of West London for five decades and is today second only to Rio's Carnival in size. Rooted in Caribbean culture, the bank holiday event is also reflective of modern London, and features static sound systems and live stages, as well as an incredible parade of "Mas" (masquerade) bands, where the wonderful themed costumes meet spectacular music and dance.

Notting Hill, London; nhcarnival.org

EGTON BRIDGE GOOSEBERRY SHOW

The Gooseberry Show is open

These juicy, tart, vitamin-C-packed fruit were at a peak of popularity in the 19th century, and amateur growing clubs, mostly in the Midlands and North of England, held competitions for the biggest and tastiest specimens. Now, just a handful of goosegog shows remain in the UK, the oldest of which was established at Egton Bridge in 1800. Each year, on the first Tuesday in August, members of the village's Old Gooseberry Society enter their biggest gooseberries into one of four classes: red, yellow, green or white. The heaviest is determined by a precise apothecary scale that measures in drams and grains. Past winners have weighed in at 33 drams – the size of a golf ball – but in 2019 a new world record was set at 36 drams, 12 grains, with a yellow "Millennium" berry. Thrilling stuff.

Egton Bridge, North Yorkshire; egtongooseberryshow.org.uk

KETTLEWELL SCARECROW FESTIVAL

Said to be the biggest of its kind in the country, this unusual festival boasts scarecrows in every nook and cranny of the village, from famous celebrities and sports stars to topical characters and the downright quirky. The local scenery is gorgeous (it appears in the opening credits of *Emmerdale*), and for the thousands of visitors that the nine-day event attracts there are delicious homemade cakes, fresh-cut sandwiches, soup, quiches and more, served all day in the village hall. Fun for all the family.

Kettlewell, North Yorkshire; kettlewellscarecrowfestival.co.uk

ROBIN HOOD FESTIVAL

Enjoyed by families and fans of the Robin Hood tales since 1984, this seven-day festival features live re-enactments, song, dance, storytelling, sword-fighting, archery and adventures with the outlaws. You'll find food and drink stalls, craft stands, demonstrations,

Hot-air balloons take to the skies in Bristol

BRISTOL INTERNATIONAL BALLOON FIESTA

The incredible sight of hundreds of hot-air balloons filling the skies above Bristol is surely one not to be missed. Europe's largest annual balloon meeting attracts more than 130 participants from across the globe, with mass ascents and night-time illuminations in time to music, plus ground-level stalls, fairground rides and plenty of entertainment. Now's the time to fulfil that lifetime ambition to book a ride in the sky.

Ashton Court Estate, Bristol; bristolballoonfiesta.co.uk

medieval music, have-a-go archery and plenty of activities that will immerse you in the legends of Sherwood Forest, famous as our hero's home.
Sherwood Forest, Nottinghamshire; visitsherwood.co.uk

ARUNDEL FESTIVAL

This free community event is one of the largest multi-arts festivals in the south. Its gallery trail is the largest walking trail in the UK, plus there's music, art, dance, drama, street entertainment, poetry, comedy, cabaret and more.
Arundel, West Sussex; arundelfestival.co.uk

THE SCARBOROUGH CRICKET FESTIVAL

One of the most historic sporting events in the world, the Scarborough Cricket Festival is an end-of-season series of cricket matches featuring Yorkshire County Cricket Club.
It has been held in Scarborough since 1876 and, with the stands built right to the boundary edge, offers exceptional views and a unique atmosphere.
Scarborough Cricket Club, Yorkshire; scarboroughcricketclub.co.uk

INTERNATIONAL BEATLEWEEK FESTIVAL

Fab Four fans converge on the Mersey for a week-long event that includes speakers, films, a giant Beatles flea market, performances from tribute bands and live music galore. Come together!
Around Liverpool; internationalbeatleweek.com

FILM4 SUMMER SCREEN

As the sun sets over the London skyline, live DJs spin a soundtrack inspired by the upcoming screening and the Edmond J. Safra Fountain Court at London's Somerset House transforms into a beautiful open-air cinema.
Just take a picnic and a cushion and enjoy the show.
Somerset House, London; somersethouse.org.uk

THE BRITISH FIREWORK CHAMPIONSHIPS

Every year, six professional firework display companies are selected by a draw to put on a ten-minute show for this spectacular two-night competition. The natural amphitheatre of Plymouth's harbour and Sound is the ideal venue for large-scale pyrotechnics, plus there's entertainment on the Hoe with a funfair, live music and food and drink.
The Hoe, Plymouth, Devon; britishfireworks.co.uk

SEPTEMBER 2021

SOMERSET CARNIVALS

The Somerset Carnivals are a tradition that dates back to at least the 1600s, when many parts of the county commemorated the Gunpowder Plot. Today, they combine open-air entertainment with fairgrounds, food and a parade of illuminated carts that is said to be the largest in the world. The carts can be over 50 feet long, and are covered in intricate, themed designs featuring moving parts and thousands of light bulbs – not to mention the characters, all played by members of the local Carnival Clubs. They visit Somerset towns on a circuit each autumn, starting in mid-September.
scuk.co.uk

GRAIL QUEST RACE

The UK's only medieval-themed obstacle race takes place on Upton Bridge Farm on the Somerset Levels. Racers take part in either an eight or 16 km race in which they must attack "Battle of >

JANE AUSTEN FESTIVAL

If you are wandering around Bath during this 10-day festival, don't be surprised to encounter characters from *Pride and Prejudice*, *Emma* or *Sense and Sensibility*. The Regency era comes to life with this annual celebration of all things Austen, which features more than 90 events, from masked balls to country dances and tours of the city to dramatic performances.
Various locations, Bath; janeaustenfestivalbath.co.uk

The Jane Austen Festival opens with a Regency-costumed promenade

The annual bonfire season on the South Coast starts in early September

SUSSEX BONFIRE SEASON

Bonfire celebrations are held around Sussex from early September until the end of November, marking both Guy Fawkes Night and the burning of local Protestant martyrs. The many Sussex bonfire societies stage impressive and atmospheric torch-lit processions through the narrow streets of these historic towns and villages, featuring burning barrels, costumed marchers, thumping drums and (sometimes controversial) giant celebrity effigies. Enormous bonfires are the focal point and everything ends with a huge firework display. There's an event every weekend and they can attract huge crowds, especially for the one in Lewes, the UK's biggest Bonfire Night celebration (always held on 5 November), so plan ahead carefully. Dress warmly, leave the car at home and be prepared for long waits, loud noises and lots of smoke.

Around Sussex; lewesbonfirecelebrations.com

> Wessex" with the courage of a medieval knight, conquer "Agincourt" and trample, crawl or swim through the trenches. A medieval village has axe-throwing, archery, weaponry displays, wholesome food and plenty of mead.

Long Sutton, Somerset; grailquestrace.co.uk

HERITAGE OPEN DAYS

See hidden places and try out new experiences in England's largest festival of history, architecture and culture. Every year in September, places across the country throw open their doors, allowing you to see inside historic homes, museum archives, castles, boats, gardens and all sorts of fascinating buildings, many of which are usually closed to the public. There are more than 5,500 free events taking place across the nation.

heritageopendays.org.uk

THE HANDMADE FESTIVAL

From heritage skills to contemporary crafts, this festival celebrates everything handmade, offering shopping, workshops and demonstrations, with more than 200 hand-picked designer/makers from around the country.

Battersea Park, London; thehandmadefestival.com

MATLOCK BATH ILLUMINATIONS

First held in 1897 to celebrate Queen Victoria's Diamond Jubilee, the Matlock Bath Illuminations is a unique floating parade that now takes place every year on weekend evenings in September and October. The display of themed models is decorated by the Matlock Bath Venetian Boat Builders' Association with thousands of coloured lights, and then mounted on rowing boats to be paraded along the River Derwent. As darkness falls, the brightly lit models appear to glide along the water by themselves. Thousands watch from the riverbanks and there are fireworks on the Saturday parades. Expect a carnival atmosphere!

Derwent Gardens, Matlock Bath, Derbyshire; derbyshiredales.gov.uk/things-to-do/whats-on/matlock-bath-illuminations

EGREMONT CRAB FAIR

Named for crab apples as opposed to crustaceans, this fair was established in 1267, making it one of the oldest in the world. Traditional events combine with modern attractions, with events starting on the Friday night with a free concert in Main Street.
The highlight of Saturday is a parade in which apples are thrown from a cart, as well as visiting

Model of Uncle Tom Cobley and all riding to Widecombe fair in Devon

WIDECOMBE FAIR

Run entirely by volunteers to raise money for local good causes, as well as providing an opportunity for farmers to compare the size of their tractors, Widecombe Fair takes place on the second Tuesday of September each year and attracts visitors from far and wide. It's the epitome of a charming country fair, with everything from tug o' war to bale tossing, a dog and duck display to the ever-popular terrier race. There's live music, vintage machinery, a handicraft and produce tent and, if you keep your eyes peeled, you might spot Uncle Tom Cobley on his grey mare.

Widecombe-in-the-Moor, Dartmoor, Devon; widecombefair.com

LUDLOW FOOD FESTIVAL

Ludlow has been described as the UK's second gourmet capital, and its annual food festival involves free talks, celebrity chef demos and tastings from more than 180 exhibitors in the grounds of Ludlow Castle.
Ludlow, Shropshire; foodfestival.co.uk

Treats from Ludlow's Food Festival which is held in the ancient castle grounds

LAST NIGHT OF THE PROMS

Are you set to sing Elgar's *Land of Hope and Glory*? The rousing song provides the traditional finale, usually on the second Saturday of September, to the series of classical concerts at the Royal Albert Hall. It's in lighter vein, with popular classics followed by a second half of patriotic pieces.
Royal Albert Hall, London; bbc.co.uk/proms

LONDON DESIGN FESTIVAL

Celebrating London as the design capital of the world and powerhouse of the creative industries, this nine-day festival encompasses hundreds of inspiring events all over the city. From Bankside to West Kensington, in a host of different venues, designers will present new ideas, new products and new ways of thinking. A variety of eye-catching public installations will also impress.
Venues across London; londondesignfestival.com

FAVERSHAM HOP FESTIVAL

Set in the beautiful medieval heart of Faversham, this lively event recalls the traditional festivities associated with the hop harvest, and celebrates the town's unrivalled hop heritage. It is now one of the largest free street festivals in the south-east, and entertainment includes live music on five stages, arts and crafts, Morris dancers, a street market, a funfair and traditional parade, as well as the Hop Blessing and special tours of Shepherd Neame, Britain's oldest brewer.
Faversham, Kent; favershamhopfestival.org

ALDEBURGH FOOD AND DRINK FESTIVAL

A jam-packed weekend of adventures celebrating the quality of local food, from tastings and demonstrations to masterclasses, talks and discussions.
Snape Maltings, Aldeburgh, Suffolk; aldeburghfoodanddrink.co.uk

Crab Fair Field for local food and craft, ferret shows, equestrian events and more. Don't miss the World Gurning Championships, in which entrants compete to pull the ugliest face, at 6 pm in the Falcon Club on Croadalla Avenue.
Egremont, Cumbria; egremontcrabfair.com

PEARLY KINGS AND QUEENS HARVEST FESTIVAL

Celebrate the harvest with the Pearly Kings and Queens of London, who will be decked out in their traditional finery of dark suits with bright pearl buttons. It's the biggest event in the Pearly calendar, and there's traditional entertainment with maypole dancing and marching bands in front of the Guildhall, before a parade through the streets to St Mary Le Bow church for a service of thanksgiving.
Guildhall, London; pearlysociety.co.uk

SHEEP DRIVE AND LIVERY FAIR

GLC Chairman Harold Mote drove a flock of sheep into the City over London Bridge in 1979, a rare privilege, which since 2013 has become more common again

In medieval times, farmers drove their sheep across London Bridge into the City of London to sell them at market. Freemen of the City were, however, excused the bridge toll. This practice had all but died out by the early 20th century, but in 2013 the Worshipful Company of Woolmen arranged for Freemen of the City and their guests to officially "drive" sheep across the bridge, once again upholding the tradition of Freemen's rights. The event was so successful that it has continued ever since, with hundreds of places selling out every year. Near the drive is a fair in which many of the City of London's ancient and modern livery companies demonstrate their trade, craft or profession with colourful and interactive displays and demonstrations, along with a variety of stalls specialising in all things wool, arts and crafts and food and drink.
London Bridge, London; sheepdrive.london

Images: Shutterstock, Getty, Alamy.

BEAUTIFUL TOWN

HARROGATE

Bettys Tea Rooms on Parliament Street in Harrogate

Looking towards the Royal Pump Rooms

Cenotaph war memorial

The ornate interior of the Turkish Baths

THE discovery of Tewit Well by William Slingsby in the late 16th-century turned Harrogate from a sleepy hamlet into a spa town. The visitors kept coming and its heyday was during the Victorian era, with the wealthy arriving to take the pungent waters, bathe and to promenade through the streets.

The town is now a genteel destination, sitting on the edge of the Yorkshire Dales with a rich variety of unique shops, galleries and antiques shops.

Its spa roots are still present in the impressive Turkish Baths, one of only seven working in the UK. The baths were restored in 2003, with further restoration in 2018, and boast some of the finest tiling and glazed brickwork.

Islamic arches and Moorish tiles decorate a steam room, plunge pool, three different hot chambers and the Frigidarium in which you begin and end your trip through the baths. There were more than 600 dry hot air baths in Britain and Ireland by the end of the 19th century, but Harrogate's were considered the finest.

As well as bathing, those seeking respite from arthritis, digestive disorders, gout and all manner of other ailments also came to take the waters. Harrogate Valley Gardens became a wonder of the natural world as 36 of Harrogate's 88 mineral wells are to be found here. It's the biggest number of natural mineral springs occurring in the smallest space in the world.

Within the gardens, there is an attractive Gothic-style building with a pointed roof, built in 1858, and known as the Old Magnesia Well Pump Room, where the Victorians would spend hours each day queuing outside to sample the unique spring water known as "the cure". The building was restored in 2015 and the gardens surrounding it boast a wide variety of shrub, flower and herbaceous beds. There are Alpine rarities in spring along with a romantic rhododendron dell, which give way to a magnificent dahlia border during late summer.

At the entrance to the gardens is the hexagonal Royal Pump Room, built in the mid-1800s. It was turned into a museum in 1953 to tell the story of Harrogate. It's a short amble to the Montpellier Quarter where you'll find a fine selection of antiques shops, galleries and boutique shops. On Parliament Street you'll find Bettys Tea Rooms. Started by a Swiss confectioner more than 100 years ago, they take influence from both Switzerland and Yorkshire.

Harrogate is the venue for the Theakston Old Peculier Crime Writing Festival, which is apt as it was central to the biggest mystery of Agatha Christie's life. She vanished in 1926, sparking an enormous manhunt. Writers Arthur Conan Doyle and Dorothy L. Sayers even joined in the search. Although Christie was found 11 days later at the Old Swan Hotel in Harrogate, mystery still surrounds her disappearance.

AVRIL LOWE

John Street with its cafés and shops

DON'T MISS

Bettys Café Tea Rooms

For afternoon tea, breakfast, lunch and an early supper. Plus takeaway cakes and gifts and their coveted speciality, the Yorkshire Fat Rascal – a scone on steroids.

1 Parliament Street, Harrogate HG1 2QU 01423 814070; bettys.co.uk

Turkish Baths

"Perfecting the art of relaxation since 1897" is the motto, and as well as baths and steam to heat, cool and cleanse to enjoy, there's a full menu of treatments that the Victorians probably wouldn't recognise.

Parliament Street, Harrogate HG1 2WH 01423 556746; turkishbathsharrogate.co.uk

RHS Harlow Carr

As well as the Harrogate Valley Gardens in town, just outside you'll find Harlow Carr, a 58-acre garden to fit snugly into its Dales landscape. As well as exquisitely designed gardens and borders to give plenty of inspiration, there's also a log maze and tea room.

Crag Lane, Harrogate HG3 1QB; 01423 565418; rhs.org.

BIRDS OF BRITAIN

Through poetry and prose, Lin Bensley celebrates the winged masters of our nation's skies

Images: Shutterstock

THE comical, clown-like and portly appearance of the puffin – also known in some parts as sea parrot – has endeared the bird to millions who otherwise pay scant regard to our avian companions. Most people who can recognise a penguin can recognise a puffin. Its similarly humorous characteristics have made it our best-loved sea bird. Cuddly toy puffins are as much a part of a child's nursery as teddy bears and flopsy bunnies, and the publisher Allen Lane even adopted the bird to launch his famous series of children's books.

For me, one of the greatest pleasures of visiting Bempton Cliffs Nature Reserve is the opportunity to observe puffins at close quarters. The bird makes its nest inside a burrow and will adopt an old rabbit's hole, or willingly excavate its own upon the grassy slopes. One chick is reared at the end of a metre-long tunnel and fed by the parents for 40 days before being left to find its own way under cover of darkness to the sea where it will spend the next three years before returning to land.

Sad to say, the future has not been looking so rosy for the puffin. Globally, numbers are in sharp decline. Overfishing, pollution and climate change have all been cited as contributing factors in depleting the stocks of sand eels and capelin upon which they depend.

Lundy island in the Bristol Channel was for centuries home to a vast puffinry, but rats introduced to the island are thought to have played a part in decimating the population. The island was once virtually the bird's birthright; the name Lundy is said to be derived from the old Norse word for puffin.

A succession of islanders have produced coins and stamps bearing the bird as the official logo. A campaign to eradicate the rats has seen a gradual increase in the numbers of breeding puffins, but whether they will escape the fate of the great auk or significantly recover remains to be seen.

THE PUFFIN

Oh, there once was a puffin
Just the shape of a muffin
And he lived on an island
In the bright blue sea!
He ate little fishes
That were most delicious . . .

From *There Once Was A Puffin* by Florence Page Jacques

THE KINGFISHER

It was the Rainbow gave thee birth,
And left thee all her lovely hues;
And, as her mother's name was Tears,
So runs it in my blood to choose
For haunts the lonely pools, and keep
In company with trees that weep.
Go you and, with such glorious hues,
Live with proud peacocks in green parks;
On lawns as smooth as shining glass,
Let every feather show its marks;
Get thee on boughs and clap thy wings
Before the windows of proud kings.

From T*he Kingfisher* by William Henry Davies

A **STREAK** of electric blue is often all we see of a kingfisher as it flashes past, skimming the surface of a stream or river, uttering its piping call.

Improbable gifts have been attributed to this exotic-looking bird, including a belief that it could predict the weather. Naturalists confirmed that many were killed and hung up in homes to indicate the direction of the wind. Greeks believed that the dried corpse of a kingfisher could ward off lightning.

According to legend, Ceyx was a Grecian king who married Alcyone. Their irreverential behaviour displeased Zeus, who sent Ceyx on a sea voyage and cast down a thunderbolt, wrecking the ship and drowning Ceyx. Alcyone, mad with grief, threw herself into the sea. The gods turned the pair into kingfishers or "halcyon birds".

Thereafter it was said that for the seven days before the winter solstice and the seven days after, the waves were calmed, allowing halcyon to brood her eggs in a nest which floated upon the ocean. The phrase "halcyon days" has since come to refer to any peaceful time.

The kingfisher nests in riverbanks, laying a clutch of glossy eggs amid a pile of fish bones. Few nests smell as odorous as that of the kingfisher. Why such a beautiful bird should choose to live in such conditions is hard to comprehend.

A**S** recently as 1925 the Rev. Theodore Wood was lamenting the relative scarcity of the goldfinch in most parts of the country. The population of this most exquisite songbird was severely depleted during the 19th century, when bird-catchers trapped them in their tens of thousands to satisfy the demands of bird-fanciers. In 1860 it was reported that 132,000 were taken at Worthing, while a keeper at the British Museum recollected that in his youth he caught 12 dozen in a morning on the former site of Paddington Station!

One of the central aims of The Society for the Protection of Birds (later the RSPB) was to stem the trade of caged birds with the passing of the Protection of Birds Act of 1880. The Act was difficult to implement, and the keeping of wild birds in captivity was not abolished until the Wildlife and Countryside Act passed in 1981.

The goldfinch has substantially recovered, and is now one of the most common visitors to our gardens. It is difficult to think there can be a more pleasing sound than a charm of goldfinches, whose tinkling, sweet chiming voices bring cheer to the dullest of days. Witnessing a flock twittering as they feed is a joyous spectacle.

In *Birds And Men*, Mark Cocker notes that the goldfinch is represented in 486 examples of Renaissance art, with the majority devoted to images of the Madonna and Child. It is used to represent, among other things, fertility, redemption and resurrection. For centuries it was also assigned curative powers and even believed to be capable of healing those afflicted by the Plague.

THE GOLDFINCH

The redcap is a painted bird
And beautiful its feathers are;
In early spring its voice is heard
While searching thistles brown and bare;
It makes a nest of mosses grey
And lines it round with thistle-down;
Five small pale spotted eggs they lay
In places never far from town.

From *The Redcap*
by John Clare

FOR centuries the British have had a close association with the mute swan: so close that the bird was known as the domestic swan during the medieval period when it was bred in captivity for the sole purpose of gracing the banqueting table. Roasted swan was a favourite of Henry III and legislation ensured the bird enjoyed the status apportioned to crown property, though ownership could be awarded to select individuals and wealthy dignitaries whose names were entered on an official list known as the Swan Roll, under the jurisdiction of the Royal Swan Master.

Birds were kept and reared in a swannery – a feature of several monastic dwellings – with their wings clipped to prevent them from straying, a practice that endured for 500 years. Swan was considered a delicacy at royal feasts, even if some found its fibrous texture difficult to digest, while certain detractors described it as having a "muddy" or "fishy mutton" taste.

It was not the refined palate but the prohibitive cost of rearing swans that eventually saw them fall out of favour, and introduction of the domesticated turkey in the mid-16th century soon proved more affordable and more appetising.

The Queen still maintains the title of the Seigneur (feudal lord) of the Swans and the traditional ceremony of swan-upping is performed annually, when all swans on the Thames between London Bridge and Henley are rounded up and ringed. The Royal Family and fellows of St Johns College, Cambridge, retain the privilege to eat swan, but thankfully none exercise that right nowadays and swan-upping is primarily enacted to record and conserve the species.

There is not a creature more elegant than the swan as it regally glides upon glassy waters. In flight the bird is equally graceful, when the soughing of its wings suggests an ethereal spirit from another realm.

THE MUTE SWAN

But now they drift on the still water,
Mysterious, beautiful;
Among what rushes will they build,
By what lake's edge or pool
Delight men's eyes when I awake some day
To find they have flown away?

From *The Wild Swans of Coole* by W.B. Yeats

THE SONG THRUSH

At once a voice rose among
The bleak twigs overhead
In a full-hearted evensong
Of joy illimited;
An aged thrush, frail, gaunt, and small,
In blast-beruffled plume,
Had chosen then to fling his soul
Upon the growing gloom.

From *The Darkling Thrush* by Thomas Hardy

THE song thrush was always known to my Norfolk-born grandmother as a mavis or throstle, though the name was also sometimes applied to the mistle thrush, just to confuse the issue. For both Chaucer and Shakespeare the names were interchangeable for a song thrush, whereas John Skelton knew it simply as "Mavis with her whistle."

It was named song thrush for good reason. It is one of our earliest songsters, and can be heard in February and continues throughout the year. Even if not quite as musical as the blackbird, its clear, fluting song consists of over 100 distinct phrases, with some of the more commonplace calls often rendered as "Did you do it? Did you do it?" While the next phrase may be interpreted as "You did – You did – You did." It is also a capable mimic and has been known to imitate trimphones, car alarms and various species of wild and domesticated birds.

I recall the thrill of finding the nests among the laurels in my grandparents' garden. These were always sturdily constructed from grasses, root and twigs, each with a perfectly smooth mud-lined cup in which were usually laid three to five eggs of a vivid greenish-blue dotted with black – more delicate than anything designed by Fabergé.

It was never any less fascinating to observe them in the churchyard nearby. I often saw them using a flint as an anvil to break open the shells of snails. The gully around the base of the church was often littered with remnants of their meals, proof of their reputation as a gardener's best friend.

LIKE many of the crow family, the magpie is often considered a bird of ill-omen. When I was young, if we happened to spy a maggie, we had to hold a coat or shirt button until we spotted a four-legged animal or bad luck would apparently befall us. The bird has engendered many similar superstitions up and down the country. The Reverend Swainson records that a Shropshire friend used to take his hat off and spit in the direction of the bird uttering, "Devil, Devil, I defy you."

The magpie has also long had a reputation as a kleptomaniac; renowned for its liking for shiny objects – as portrayed by Rossini in his opera *The Thieving Magpie* and more recently in the BBC sitcom *The Detectorists*.

The first part of the birds name is an abbreviated form of Margaret derived from the French equivalent, *Margot la pie*, while the second syllable may refer to its pied black and white plumage which may be perceived as a combination of good and evil.

The magpie is highly intelligent, and is one of the few non-mammals that is able to recognise itself in a mirror. Like all crows, it is extremely inquisitive. A pair used to visit my mother's garden whenever her cat was sunning itself upon the lawn.

Frisky (who was anything but) would sprawl upon the grass and lazily swish his tail until one or other of the magpies, unable to resist, would hop ever closer to nip the proffered bait and hastily make its escape before the cat could so much as move a muscle in response. Due to its playful nature it was kept by some as a pet and could easily be taught to master words and whole sentences while others kept it with poultry to warn of predators or intruders.

THE MAGPIE

One for sorrow,
Two for joy,
Three for a girl,
Four for a boy,
Five for silver,
Six for gold,
Seven for a secret,
Never to be told,
Eight for a wish,
Nine for a kiss,
Ten for a bird
You must not miss.

Traditional nursery rhyme

THE SKYLARK

Hail to thee, blithe spirit!
Bird thou never wert,
That from Heaven, or near it
Pourest thy full heart
In profuse strains of
unpremeditated art.

From *To A Skylark*
by Percy Bysshe Shelley

FEW birds are more familiar to the public at large than famed songster the skylark. Even if rather drab in appearance, the bird is emblematic of open countryside and farmland, thanks to its habit of taking to the air and soaring almost vertically to deliver its rich, loud song that George Meredith fittingly described in his poem *The Lark Ascending* as that "silver chain of sound. Of many links without a break". Inspired by the poem, Vaughan Williams composed his rapturous work of the same name and did more to popularise the bird and its song than all the versifiers and nature writers.

It is difficult to believe that the lark was once prized as a cage bird and it is hard to imagine a more callous treatment for such an aerial chorister. There is an old Norfolk saying that if one wants to hear what the lark has to say, then one should lie down in a field and listen – sound advice I have sought to follow. I have also tramped many a mile over marshland in search of skylark nests, which are remarkably difficult to locate as the parent always alights or arises some distance from the nest site. Constructed of roots and grass, sometimes lined with hair and placed in a slight hollow upon the ground, the nest is often hidden by a tussock of grass, where, for all its simplicity, it is surprisingly well camouflaged.

Intensive and inappropriate farming practices have decimated the lark population. To enlist farmers in a conservation programme will require funding from the public purse if we wish to hark back to the lark as he hangs upon the morning air, singing his song of exaltation halfway between heaven and earth.

THERE can be few who would argue that the nightingale is not one of our most welcome summer visitors, even if not for its appearance. As Bill Oddie explains, "You don't want to see a nightingale, actually, because if you do you'll be disappointed. It's just a little brown bird, and maybe that helps with the mystique of them as well – you don't see it, just hear the song."

The nightingale's rich vocalisations have captured our imagination, and inspired poets from Peter of Blois to John Keats and Edward Thomas to Paolo Garcia.

One study, as reported in the *Birds of the Western Paleartic*, revealed that an individual male possessed 250 different phrases comprising 600 basic sound-units. Each performance is unique. While the nightingale sings by day, it is at night that he comes into his own.

Between 1924 and the outbreak of World War II, cellist Beatrice Harrison gave a series of recitals with the nightingales in her Surrey garden. A million people across the world tuned in to listen to the first broadcast. The last recording featured Harrison duetting with a nightingale as bombers droned overhead.

Author Jeremy Mynott discloses: "As the crescendo of noise builds up from the bombers, so the crescendo of noise builds up from the nightingale – and it's the most dramatic combination of sounds."

Izaak Walton declared the nightingale "breathes such sweet loud music out of her little instrumental throat that it might make mankind to think miracles are not ceased."

Who could disagree with such a statement?

THE NIGHTINGALE

But never elsewhere in one
place I knew
So many nightingales; and
far and near,
In wood and thicket, over the
wide groove,
They answer and provoke
each other's song
With skirmish and capricious
passagings,
And murmurs musical and
swift jug jug,
And one low piping sound
more sweet than all
Stirring the air with such a
harmony

From *The Nightingale*
by Samuel Taylor Coleridge

PEOPLE are often surprised to see a barn owl hunting in the daylight hours. The bird was very much associated with darkness and graveyards and thereby gained a sinister persona, regarded by some as a portent of death. In my youth I climbed many church towers in the days when louvred openings were invariably neglected, to find the nests of barn owls among ancient cross beams and bell-frames. I would agree with the naturalist W.H. Hudson who declared, "The barn-owl takes up his abode by preference in a building of some kind – an old ruin, a loft in a barn or an outhouse: but above most sites he prefers an ivyclad church-tower . . ."

The bird's night-time howls and shrieks once alarmed more superstitious communities, as Gilbert White recorded when he heard of whole villages "up in arms on such an occasion, imagining the church-yard to be full of goblins and spectres."

Unlike all other owls, the barn owl has always displayed a strong inclination to roost and nest in man-made structures. A strange choice when one considers that the birds were once so roundly condemned by gamekeepers and farmers alike, who persecuted them to extremes and shot and trapped them in their thousands.

Specimens were nailed to barn doors with outspread wings to warn the world that this feathered pest would not be tolerated.

THE BARN OWL

When cats run home and light is come,
And dew is cold upon the ground,
And the far off stream is dumb,
And the whirring sail goes round,
And the whirring sail goes round;
Alone and warming his five wits,
The white owl in the belfry sits.

From *The Owl*
by Alfred Lord Tennyson

Attitudes to wildlife have changed for the better over recent decades. A local farmer has been only too happy for me to erect an owl box in his disused drainage mill. Several broods, I am pleased to say, have been reared there over the years and the only persecution they suffer now is from the occasional kestrel stealing the parent birds' quarry as they return to feed their raucous owlets.

THE WREN

The quick note of the russet wren,
Familiar to the haunts of men,
He quits in hollow'd wall his bow'r,
And thro' the winter's gloomy hour
Sings cheerily: nor yet hath lost
His blitheness, chill'd by pinching frost . . .

From *The British Months*
by Bishop Mant

IN my youth, hardly a year went by without a wren building its nest within the hollowed timbers of our open-fronted cart shed. In some years two nests would appear almost simultaneously, and I soon came to realise that the male constructs a series of nests, up to half a dozen, in his efforts to attract a female.

In winter months, the bird being highly susceptible to prolonged cold snaps, these nests would on occasion serve as communal roosts and I recall finding up to eight or nine birds in one nest. But records of 60 or more have not been uncommon, and they are equally willing to seek refuge in the disused nests of other birds or squirrel dreys.

Ever active, it flits here and there with fitful movements and permanently elevated tail, its shrill, trilling song uncannily vociferous for a bird of such diminutive stature. There is something eminently captivating about the wren's alert behaviour which has made it one of the nation's favourites.

Dear Jenny wren was, however, not always quite so beloved. Once, the custom of Hunting the Wren (also called wrenning) was practised throughout much of the country. According to legend, the wren betrayed the hiding place of St Stephen to his persecutors and every 26 December it was ritually hunted and, emulating the fate of the martyr, stoned to death as a form of revenge.

Celtic pagans were supposed to regard the wren as sacred and believed its utterances to be omnipotent, while the druids considered it a bird of prophesy. In Ireland the bird was once known as a magician or magus and the Welsh word for wren is *dryw* meaning seer. I, for one, am willing to acknowledge the wranny as the king of birds.

Milk for school children, 1955

MILK OF HUMAN KINDNESS

This year marks the 75th anniversary of the introduction of school milk. Richard Ginger looks back

Images: Mary Evans Picture Library, Shutterstock

FOR countless people of a certain age reminiscing about their early years at school, it's highly likely that most will recall the clink and rattle that heralded the arrival of mid-morning crates of milk in the classroom.

In an unreconstructed age before girl power and Women's Lib overturned such roles, this daily delivery was unquestionably deemed man's work. Thus, one or two plucky young boys, red-faced and with chests proudly puffed out, took on the task of mini milkmen, hefting the heavy crates as part of their hunter-gatherers-in-the-making training. The girls, no doubt, couldn't help but swoon at this impressive display of unbridled masculine vigour.

Once they were delivered and foil top peeled open, for some 10 minutes or so a relative silence was only interrupted by the occasional glug, slurp, comical burp (triggering much delighted sniggering) and inevitable spillage. Finally, with the backs of small hands having been satisfyingly wiped across milk-slathered chops (leaving the ubiquitous milk moustaches in place), the school lessons once again commenced.

The provision of universal free milk in school was introduced in August 1946. During an era of ongoing food rationing, the post-war Labour government wanted to make all meals free to "raise the standards of the nation's health", but due to the potential escalating costs of such a venture finally settled on the white stuff.

Rich in calcium, protein and nutrients, milk was seen as the perfect power drink for boosting kids' energy and building a generation with strong, healthy teeth and bones. In the coming decades milk also gained a slightly different reputation largely thanks

Dr Hilary Jones is a GP, TV presenter and spokesperson for The School & Nursery Milk Alliance

Dr Hilary Jones

My memories of school milk as a child are that it wasn't always the most appealing thing, as I'm sure many of my peers will agree. But I take the benefits of drinking milk in school with me to this day. Drinking a glass of the white stuff is one of the closest things to a full package of all the nutrients you need. The days of questionable milk are now gone, in part thanks to the campaigning of the School & Nursery Milk Alliance, as education settings are encouraged to offer milk fresh, chilled and as a mid-morning snack to ensure maximum benefits: reducing hunger, getting children the nutrients and the habits they need to stay healthy as they grow.

Research states quite clearly that milk is an unmatched nutritional powerhouse, containing calcium, potassium, protein, phosphorus, vitamin B12, and riboflavin: practically everything a growing child needs. The unrivalled content in milk helps maintain strong bones and protect against tooth decay, and as a healthy option for satiety it helps to tackle and prevent child obesity. Milk's vitamins and minerals can aid the concentration and attention of young minds in the classroom. All this combines to make this British institution a must for children as we face some of the health issues facing our youngsters today.

to comedian Benny Hill's creation, Ernie, the fastest milkman in the west, who served up daily portions (nudge-nudge, wink-wink) to lusty and lonely housewives. Meanwhile, celebrities such as Barbara Windsor, Sid James and Muhammad Ali all lined up to prove it packed a punch in advertising campaigns of the time.

However, despite its health-giving merits, not all toddlers in school looked forward to their daily tot of full fat, creamy goodness in its third-of-a-pint bottle. While other classmates lapped it up with all the eagerness of a stray tabby, they were like contestants in some early version of a Bushtucker Trial. The summer months were particularly bad, with the milk delivered early and left outside to gently curdle in the sun, it meant they grimaced their way through the warm and thickening liquid beneath the watchful eyes of teachers.

However, for those who couldn't stomach their daily intake of cow juice, an unlikely saviour was to appear on the horizon in September 1970. As the Secretary of State for Education and Science in Edward Heath's Conservative government, Margaret Thatcher put forward a package to save £200 million from the education budget, part of which included the end of free milk to schoolchildren aged seven to eleven.

The future PM received a proper hand-bagging for her efforts from political opponents and the media alike, instantly becoming about as popular as the child-catcher in *Chitty Chitty Bang Bang*, complete with her own pantomimic moniker that rang out in playgrounds across the land: "Thatcher, Thatcher, Milk Snatcher". She later recalled in her autobiography, "I learned a valuable lesson. I had incurred the maximum of political odium for the minimum of political benefit". The crates in the classroom fell silent as a generation of older primary-school kids were instantly freed from free milk.

Today, free milk is still available to thousands of smaller children under the age of five, alongside those receiving or entitled to free school meals. It's also subsidised for all other children in primary education. However, the British imperial system third-of-a-pint measure is now served up (for how long?) in an EU-friendly daily portion of 189 milky millilitres. Similarly, full fat has been traded in for semi-skimmed. And in an age of plant-based alternatives, ranging from oat to soya milk, who knows if the drink will still be in classrooms for its 150th anniversary or if it will finally be put out to pasture?

This England took to Twitter to find out what memories people had of getting their daily dose of milk at school.

@parkerdairies It was always warm, even in winter! We now supply semi-skimmed milk in 189 ml cartons to 366 schools in London, around 21,000 pints per week. Ours is always cold and tastes lovely.

@SallyShorthose It was in warm, tetrahedron cartons and tasted a bit like sick, but being milk monitor was a great honour. I missed it when it had gone. One of my friends rather precociously challenged Mrs T on a radio show, and our teachers sucked through their teeth about "political parents".

@CroPage In the freezing winter of 1962-3 it froze in its little bottles outside our Nissen hut classroom. We had to put them on the radiators to defrost. The result was . . . Ew!

School milk supply

Colin Firth with Helena Bonham Carter as?

Golf caddy Oddjob, played by Harold Sakata with boss Goldfinger (Gert Frobe)

GREAT BRITISH FILM QUIZ

Test your knowledge of classic films with our brain-teasing quiz

1. Which tongue-tied British monarch, played by Colin Firth, was the subject of 2010's *The King's Speech?*

2. Mike Leigh's 1999 film *Topsy-Turvy* told the story of which real-life musical duo?

3. Which English actress was Oscar-nominated for her role as an embittered military wife who has a passionate affair with Burt Lancaster in *From Here to Eternity*?

4. For which 1939 film did Robert Donat win an Oscar for his role as a beloved schoolmaster looking back at his life and marriage?

5. Which well-known author wrote the play on which the classic 1945 romance *Brief Encounter* was based?

6. The 2018 comedy *The Favourite* starred which English actress as the troubled 18th-century monarch, Queen Anne?

7. In which 1949 Ealing comedy did residents of a London borough discover they were really a Burgundian principality and therefore exempt from post-war rationing?

8. In the 1964 Bond film *Goldfinger*, what is the villain Oddjob's unique weapon of choice?

9. Which British director made his feature film debut with *Truly, Madly, Deeply* before going on to win best director Oscar for *The English Patient*?

10. Which internationally acclaimed British ballet dancer and actress is best remembered for her performance in the 1948 classic *The Red Shoes*?

11. In which 1948 gangster film did Richard Attenborough play psychopathic south coast thug Pinkie Brown?

Juliet Stevenson as Nina in Truly, Madly Deeply. *But who was the director?*

Richard Attenborough and Carol Marsh in?

The car in full flight: who played the lead?

Richard Burton and Olivia de Havilland

12. For which British film did Maggie Smith win a best actress Oscar in 1969?

13. Who starred as the great English painter JMW Turner in the 2014 drama, *Mr Turner*?

14. Who wrote the novel on which Stanley Kubrick's 1971 film *A Clockwork Orange* was based?

15. Which British heartthrob played Richard Hannay in Alfred Hitchcock's 1935 classic thriller *The 39 Steps*?

16. Can you name the English heavyweight boxer famous for striking the gong that introduced J. Arthur Rank films?

David Niven and Kim Hunter in which wartime romance?

17. In which Oscar-winning 1968 Dickens adaptation does the song *Food, Glorious Food* feature?

18. Which English actress took on the role of Truly Scrumptious in *Chitty Chitty Bang Bang* after it was turned down by Julie Andrews?

19. Who played ruthless London mobster Harold Shand in the brutal 1980 gangster movie *The Long Good Friday*?

20. Glenda Jackson won two best actress Oscars – for *A Touch of Class* (1973) and which earlier film in 1969?

21. Which British film company, founded in 1934, is best known for the hit horror films it made from the late 1950s through to the 1970s?

22. Richard Burton got his big break playing opposite Olivia de Havilland in a 1952 adaptation of which Daphne du Maurier novel?

23. Which English actor played buttoned-up police sergeant Neil Howie in the cult horror film *The Wicker Man*?

24. In which classic 1949 comedy did Alec Guinness play nine different members of the same upper-class family, the D'Ascoynes?

25. Who directed the 1982 film *The Draughtsman's Contract*?

26. In what classic 1971 crime thriller does Michael Caine play a gangster returning to his roots on Tyneside?

27. In which spirit-rousing wartime Shakespeare adaptation does Laurence Olivier cry: "Once more unto the breach, dear friends . . ."?

28. Which award-strewn English director won best-film Baftas for *Odd Man Out*, *The Fallen Idol* and *The Third Man*, and a best director Oscar for *Oliver!*?

29. Which wartime romance stars David Niven as an RAF pilot trying to fly his damaged bomber home with the help of a radio operator with whom he falls in love?

30. Name the rock star who played a prominent role in Nicolas Roeg's 1970 crime drama *Performance*?

31. The inhumane treatment of British POWs forced to build a railway line in Burma was the subject of which 1957 film?

32. Which *Coronation Street* actress had an early starring role as Cleopatra in *Carry On Cleo*?

This incompetent inspector was played by?

Leigh and Brando in which film?

Anthony Hopkins was the uptight butler in?

33. Which English actor became world famous for playing an incompetent French police inspector in which film series?

34. Which 1951 Ealing comedy stars Alec Guinness and Stanley Holloway as a pair of amateur crooks planning a bullion heist?

35. Who played Sherlock Holmes in Terence Fisher's classic 1959 adaptation of *The Hound of the Baskervilles*?

36. The Beatles' George Harrison met his future wife Pattie Boyd in 1964 on the set of the band's first film. What was it called?

37. Which British actor won an Oscar for his title performance in the 1983 hit *Gandhi*?

38. Who directed the much-loved 1969 Barnsley-based film about a boy and his bird, *Kes*?

39. British actress Vivien Leigh won two best actress Oscars, for *Gone with the Wind* in 1939 and which other film 12 years later?

40. *Room at the Top* starring Laurence Harvey was a huge British hit in 1959. But who was the French actress who won an Oscar for her role as Harvey's married lover?

41. Which actor got his big break playing the title role in the 1962 box-office smash *Lawrence of Arabia*?

42. Which actor played against type as the snobbish, upper-class Lieutenant Gonville Bromhead in the 1964 film *Zulu*?

43. In what year did *The Belles of St Trinian's* first appear on screen?

44. Which actress ruled in the regal title role in 2006 film *The Queen*?

45. Which English author and diarist wrote the stage play on which the 1994 hit *The Madness of King George* was based?

46. Which 1993 film adaptation starred Anthony Hopkins as an uptight butler in an English stately home?

47. Which English author wrote the short story on which the 1973 thriller *Don't Look Now*, starring Donald Sutherland and Julie Christie, was based?

48. In Bruce Robinson's 1987 black comedy *Withnail and I*, which accomplished character actor played the unforgettable Uncle Monty?

HM the Queen was played by which national treasure?

49. Which Wigan-born comedian was Britain's highest-paid homegrown screen star of the late 1930s and early 1940s?

50. Which great British crime caper ends literally in a cliffhanger, with a bus teetering over a cliff in the Alps, and a pile of stolen gold sliding towards the rear doors?

To see how you got on, turn to page 106 for answers.

LANDMARKS OF ENGLAND CROSSWORD

ACROSS

8 County in which you would find the White Cliffs of Dover (4)
9 Town near the sculpture The Angel of the North (9)
10 Haworth Parsonage family name (6)
11 19th-century Prime Minister, whose family seat was Howick Hall in Northumberland (4,4)
12 Thomas ___, historian whose London house in Cheyne Row is owned by the National Trust (7)
14 Torquay museum with a recreated Victorian street scene that opened in 1987 (7)
17 Traditional rowing vessel, featured in *Three Men in a Boat* (5)
18 Building in Gloucester used to depict Hogwarts in several *Harry Potter* films (9)
21 Name given to the River Thames in and near to Oxford (4)
23 Artistic medium, as seen at the significant Arts and Crafts property Red House at Bexleyheath (5)
24 The ___, inlet of the North Sea between Norfolk and Lincolnshire (4)
25 Soldier outside Buckingham Palace, for instance (9)
27 Sand ___, peninsula in Poole Harbour, Dorset (5)
30 Somerset gorge (7)
32 ___ Lane, site of the onset of the Great Fire of London (7)
34 Coughton Court in Warwickshire was associated with a famous plot that took place in this month (8)
36 Sherwood ___, legendary Nottinghamshire home of Robin Hood (6)
38 Cornish town associated with the mining of clay (2,7)
39 The ___ Bridge, structure over the River Severn at Shropshire (4)

DOWN

1 Enclosure of pasture land for antlered animals, such as at Petworth House in West Sussex (4,4)
2 Famous public school near Windsor (4)
3 Sci-fi author to whom there is a Martian sculpture dedicated in Woking, Surrey (1,1,5)
4 Product for which Sheffield is famous (5)
5 Bird of prey that was reintroduced to Rutland Water in the 1990s (6)
6 Influential pottery manufacturer with a museum in Stoke-on-Trent inscribed in UNESCO's UK Memory of the World Register (8)
7 Alderley ___, affluent village in Cheshire with a dramatic sandstone escarpment (4)
13 Seven boat ___ were constructed on the Grand Western Canal in Somerset, predating the one at Anderton (5)
15 Mary Anne ___, writer buried at Highgate Cemetery (5)
16 Roman emperor associated with a wall in northern England (7)
19 ___ Crag, most famous fell in Cumbria's Lakeland (4)
20 Mischievous beings associated with Lincoln's iconic place of worship (4)
22 ___ Downs, Britain's newest National Park (5)
24 Area of SE England (5)
26 Ancient trackway, described as Britain's oldest road (8)
28 Part of the name of two towns – one on the River Thames and one on the River Hull (8)
29 County that is home to Framlingham Castle (7)
31 Female superior such as Hilda, associated with the site on which Whitby Abbey stands (6)
33 Midlands area, the main setting for Shakespeare's *As You Like It* (5)
35 Traditional structure for drying hops (4)
37 Building such as Corfe Castle or Witley Court (4)

Extract from
Ode to the West Wind

By Percy Bysshe Shelley

Make me thy lyre, even as the forest is:
What if my leaves are falling like its own!
The tumult of thy mighty harmonies
Will take from both a deep, autumnal tone,
Sweet though in sadness. Be thou, Spirit fierce,
My spirit! Be thou me, impetuous one!
Drive my dead thoughts over the universe
Like withered leaves, to quicken a new birth!
And, by the incantation of this verse,
Scatter, as from an unextinguished hearth
Ashes and sparks, my words among mankind!
Be through my lips to unawakened earth
The trumpet of a prophecy! O Wind,
If Winter comes, can Spring be far behind?

Winter at Snape Maltings, Suffolk

AUTUMN TO WINTER

Events including Lumiere Durham, the best-dressed stately homes, classic British food, plus the history of the Christmas pudding >

From the World Conker Championships to award-winning Christmas markets, Katherine Sorrell recommends some of the best winter events

THE GREAT FRAMLINGHAM SAUSAGE FESTIVAL

All hail to the great British banger! This one-day festival celebrates the great sausages made in East Anglia using local ingredients and mouth-watering recipes. Sausage makers take over the whole town of Framlingham, sizzling their produce, from Cumberland to chorizo, for you to try. There are also food stands, live music, workshops and children's events. The festival even has its own mascot – Teddie the sausage dog, of course.
Framlingham, Suffolk.
framlinghamsausagefestival.com

The sizzling sausage is celebrated in Framlingham

TENTERDEN FOLK FESTIVAL

This friendly festival takes place over four days, including the first Saturday of October, celebrating folk song, music, dance, crafts and traditions. As well as the main concerts and special shows, there are lively English barn dances, sing-a-rounds, music sessions and workshops, and don't miss the procession of Morris sides and other folk dance display teams on the Saturday.
Tenterden, Kent.
tenterdenfolkfestival.org.uk

DARTMOUTH FOOD FESTIVAL

Dartmouth's Food Festival takes place towards the end of October, featuring cooking contests, classes and demonstrations by celebrity chefs and local cookery heroes, drinks seminars and tastings, food and drink stalls, street entertainers and a host of fun children's activities.
Dartmouth, Devon.
dartmouthfoodfestival.com

Interesting foods to explore

BIRMINGHAM COMEDY FESTIVAL

From Michael McIntyre to Jimmy Carr, some huge names have appeared at this ten-day, city-wide extravaganza. Stand-up is at its core, but you can also enjoy cabaret, improv, music, puppet shows, film screenings, poetry readings and more.
Venues across Birmingham. bhamcomfest.co.uk

RUGBY LEAGUE WORLD CUP

The Rugby League World Cup is contested every four years, and 2021 will be the first time in the sport's history that the men's, women's and wheelchair world cups will be taking place simultaneously. The tournament kicks off on 23 October at St James's Park, Newcastle, with the opening ceremony and first England men's game against Samoa, and continues until the finals on 27 November.
Old Trafford, Manchester. rlwc2021.com

BATTLE OF HASTINGS RE-ENACTMENT

The Battle of Hastings is re-enacted

Get up close and personal to one of the most important battles in English history: the Battle of Hastings. English Heritage's biggest and most popular event of the year attracts an audience of thousands to watch armies clash on the very spot where King Harold and William, Duke of Normandy, fought in 1066. There's plenty more on offer in this lively weekend, too: visit the encampments of Norman and Saxon soldiers and discover what life was like in an 11th-century army; see the weapons, armour and clothing worn by Saxon and Norman soldiers; meet falconers and their majestic birds of prey, or simply take a wander down the medieval traders' row for a special souvenir.
Battle, East Sussex. english-heritage.org.uk

CHELTENHAM LITERATURE FESTIVAL

One of the oldest literary events in the world, established in 1949, the Literature Festival at Cheltenham presents more than 600 of the world's finest writers, actors, politicians, poets and leading opinion-formers to celebrate the joys of the written word. During the ten-day programme, visitors to the beautiful spa town are able to take part in an impressive programme of around 500 debates, interviews and workshops, plus Book It!, a mini festival within a festival for families and young readers.
Cheltenham, Gloucestershire. cheltenhamfestivals.com/literature

BFI LONDON FILM FESTIVAL

Head to the London Film Festival for a two-week showcase of the best in contemporary world cinema – from documentaries and animation to experimental films and the latest big releases. There will be premieres, galas, talks and debates, book signings, free screenings and other special events. Make sure to check their booking policies online before you go.
Various venues across central London. bfi.org.uk

HORSE OF THE YEAR SHOW

Billed as the biggest week of the year for equestrian entertainment, the Horse of the Year Show offers thrilling competitions and breathtaking displays of horsemanship, including the finals to many national showjumping championships as well as the chance to get up close and meet some of the horses themselves.
NEC, Birmingham. hoys.co.uk

GREAT NORTHERN CONTEMPORARY CRAFT FAIR

The North's foremost contemporary craft fair features more than 150 designer/makers, from recent graduates to highly respected names, all selected for their excellence and selling to the public over the course of four days.
Victoria Baths, Hathersage, Manchester. greatnorthernevents.co.uk

WINTER DROVING

Turn back your clock four centuries: this festival is a Cumbrian cultural event that harks back to the tradition of herding animals over long distances to market – though these days it has plenty of modern twists. A celebration of all things rural, the >

WORLD CONKER CHAMPIONSHIPS

Apparently, if you carry a conker in your pocket it helps prevent piles and rheumatism. Or you might want to use it to play a good old-fashioned game of conkers instead. How about entering a team into the World Conker Championships, held in the village of Southwick, Northamptonshire, on the second Sunday of October each year? Organised by Ashton Conker Club, the competition has taken place since 1965, when some friends were trying to find something to do after their fishing trip was rained off. These days thousands come to watch the event in the grounds of a local pub, and entrants jet in from around the world, with competitions for both adults and juniors. There's entertainment, too, and plenty of money raised for the visually impaired.
Shuckburgh Arms, Southwick, Northamptonshire. worldconkerchampionships.com

Power dressing: conker championships

NOTTINGHAM GOOSE FAIR

The annual travelling fair, which has a history going back more than 700 years, returns to Nottingham every year in October, featuring more than 500 family attractions, from all-time classics to new, white-knuckle experiences. It's one of the largest funfairs in the UK, and gets its name from the days when traders would march their geese to the famous Nottingham market to be sold just in time for the Michaelmas celebrations. Don't miss the fair's trademark meal of minty mushy peas.
Nottingham, Nottinghamshire. visit-nottinghamshire.co.uk/whats-on

The Goose Fair in the Market Place in Nottingham, 1907

> festival includes a food and craft market, street performers, a vintage fun fair, live music, fancy dress for dogs, traditional games on the village green and a torch-lit procession which features fire, drumming, giant lanterns and participants wearing animal masks.
Penrith, Cumbria. edenarts.co.uk

TRAFALGAR DAY

The most important day in the naval calendar, and one that defined British sailing for hundreds of years, Trafalgar Day commemorates Admiral Lord Nelson's victory over a combined French and Spanish fleet at the Battle of Trafalgar on 21 October, 1805. In Portsmouth, a ceremony takes place on board the warship HMS Victory, Nelson's flagship at the Battle of Trafalgar, while in London, on the closest Sunday to the 21st, hundreds of Sea Cadets demonstrate their skills and march in formation down The Mall towards Buckingham Palace – a stirring sight.
Central London. sea-cadets.org

Ripe for the picking at the Killerton Estate in Devon

APPLE DAY

Apple Day celebrations take place throughout the country on 21 October, raising awareness not only of the importance of orchards to our landscape and culture, but also of the provenance and traceability of food. See and try hundreds of different apples, many of them varieties not sold in regular shops, buy apple dishes and drinks, ask the "apple doctor" for advice and identify the tree in your garden. Search local listings for events near you, or try one of the following:

• Celebrate the 2,200 varieties of apple in the national fruit collection at the National Apple Festival at Brogdale Collections, Kent, with a guided walking or tractor tour of the orchards, baking, talks, artisan food, music and a miniature railway. **brogdalecollections.org**
• Wander among the apple trees of Sparrow Park Orchard, Killerton, Devon, and enjoy local craft stalls, storytelling and live music, and collect fallen apples to turn into your own juice.
nationaltrust.org.uk/killerton
• Taste a wide variety of the old and new apples and pears grown at Blackmoor Estate, Hampshire, with a rural craft fair and demonstrations, community fete, local produce, horse and cart rides, Morris dancing and cider.
blackmoorestate.co.uk
• In the walled garden at Fulham Palace, West London, the orchard will be celebrated with displays and tastings, live music, bee keeping demonstrations and children's activities.
fulhampalace.org
• The Big Apple is the annual harvest-time celebration of all things apple at Much Marcle in Herefordshire, featuring tours of cider, perry and fruit-juice makers, an apple market, talks on orchards and fruit, music, Morris dancing and more. **bigapple.org.uk**

ARMISTICE DAY

At 11 am on the 11th day of the 11th month, the nation holds a two-minute silence to remember those who gave their lives in war. Armistice is Latin for "to stand (still) arms", and this day commemorates the agreement, begun at 11 am on 11 November, 1918, to end the fighting in World War I. The National Service of Remembrance at The Cenotaph in London, attended by senior members of the Royal Family and the government, and involving a march-past of up to 10,000 veterans, is held on Remembrance Sunday, the closest Sunday to 11 November. These famous lines are from the poem *For the Fallen* by Laurence Binyon:

They shall grow not old, as we that are left grow old,
Age shall not weary them, nor the years condemn,
At the going down of the sun and in the morning,
We will remember them.

britishlegion.org.uk

Poppy wreaths at The Cenotaph, London, for Remembrance Day

LONDON TO BRIGHTON VETERAN CAR RUN

On the first Sunday in November more than 400 splendid old automobiles, all built before 1905, take part in the RAC's annual extravaganza, starting in Hyde Park and (hopefully) chugging all the way along the 60-mile route to a grand finish in Brighton.

veterancarrun.com

Vintage cars compete in the London to Brighton Veteran Car Run

The National Trust staff and volunteers create an impressive 60ft garland

CHRISTMAS FLOWER GARLAND

A highlight of the year at Cotehele, the National Trust's Tudor house in Cornwall, is the making of an enormous garland comprising tens of thousands of colourful dried flowers. The 60-ft swag is on display in the Great Hall from late November until the end of December.

Cotehele, Nr Saltash, Cornwall. nationaltrust.org.uk/cotehele

GUY FAWKES FESTIVAL AND FIREWORKS

This action-packed spectacular, held over a weekend in early November, combines science, history, activities, food and drink and – of course – an incredible display of fireworks. Relive the story of the plot with the Ghost of Guy Fawkes theatre show, too.

Royal Gunpowder mills, Waltham Abbey, Essex.
royalgunpowdermills.com

LEWES BONFIRE NIGHT CELEBRATIONS

Held on 5 November each year, this is one of the biggest celebrations in the country. Thousands turn up to watch six different celebrations scattered across the town with parades, flame torches and barrel rolling. Some fans book to stay year after year, others find it all a bit much.

Lewes, East Sussex.
lewesbonfirecelebrations.com

>

> ## SOULCAKING

The ancient tradition of soulcaking, or souling, takes place in some parts of Cheshire at Halloween and over the following two weeks, with the group in Antrobus having one of the longest histories. The mummers, all men, perform a riotous folk play involving the Black Prince, King George, the Doctor and Dick the Wild Horse, with proceeds going to charity.

Antrobus Arms and other local pubs, Antrobus, Cheshire.

THE WORLD'S BIGGEST LIAR

Do you enjoy telling a tall tale? Every November, in honour of 19th-century publican Will Ritson, who was renowned for his, ahem, "true" stories, a riveting contest is held to award the title of the biggest liar in the world. You'll have about five minutes to tell the biggest and most convincing porkie pie, with no scripts or prompt cards, and the prize is a much-coveted trophy, tie and beanie hat. Politicians, by the way, are considered professionals and so barred from entering.

The Bridge Inn, Santon Bridge, Holmrook, Cumbria. santonbridgeinn.com/the-worlds-biggest-liar

SOUTHWOLD LITERATURE FESTIVAL

Each November Ways With Words runs a literature festival in the lovely seaside resort of Southwold, Suffolk, a popular retreat for artists and writers. Besides imbibing the literary atmosphere, you can relax with excellent wine and beers at the various Adnams' Hotels in the town, be blown on the beach beside the winter sea or buy fresh fish from the harbour, where you can take the small ferry across to Walberswick. Visit the impressive St Edmund's church with its Southwold Jack, or simply take a stroll along the town's quirky pier.

Southwold, Suffolk. wayswithwords.co.uk

LUMIÈRE DURHAM AND OTHER WINTER LIGHT FESTIVALS

One plus of shorter evenings is the growing number of dazzling light displays illuminating cities, towns and historic venues up and down the country each winter. The biggest is Lumière in Durham, which takes place biannually (on the odd year) in November and attracts both local and international light artists, as well as hundreds of thousands of visitors. Other notable illuminated displays include those at Longleat, Kew Gardens, Canary Wharf, the National Arboretum at Westonbirt and a variety of English Heritage's historic properties.

The Lord Mayor's Show

THE LORD MAYOR'S SHOW

A fixture of London life for more than 800 years, the Lord Mayor's Show has its origins in King John's issue of a Royal Charter that allowed the city of London to elect its own mayor each year. A condition was that the mayor should travel upriver to Westminster and swear loyalty to the King. The mayor's journey was the celebrity spectacle of its day, and over the years it has featured in the plays of Shakespeare, the diaries of Pepys and the adventures of James Bond as well as, of course, the pantomime story of Dick Whittington (who really was the Mayor of London three times). The show was the first outside event ever to be broadcast live on television, and still has a TV audience of millions. These days, marching bands, military detachments, carriages, dance troupes, inflatables, giant contraptions and ceremonial displays combine in the joyful procession. After you've seen everybody pass, head to Paternoster Square for more live music, fairground rides and food, or to St Paul's Cathedral, which is free to enter on the day of the show.

lordmayorsshow.london

Bath Christmas Market is one of the best

CHRISTMAS MARKETS

November sees the start of the Christmas market season, an opportunity to shop for gifts and produce in a festive atmosphere. Enjoy carol singing and other live entertainment, mulled wine and roasted chestnuts, fairground rides and even ice-skating. Some are locally focused while others aim to replicate the atmosphere of traditional continental markets; look out for artisanal food and drink, hand-made products and plenty of seasonal cheer. Markets are held up and down the country, but some of the biggest include:

- Winter Wonderland at Hyde Park: a fairground atmosphere with markets, rides, attractions, shows, live music and Santa Land, plus the UK's largest open-air ice rink. **hydeparkwinterwonderland.com**
- Christkindelmarkt Leeds: a traditional German-style market featuring a scenic winter village with authentic wooden chalet stalls, a traditional carousel and daily programme of light entertainment. **millsqleeds.com/christmasmarket**
- Bath Christmas Market: an award-winning market in which local makers and designers showcase their artisan gifts within 150 twinkling chalets spread out across Bath's stunning Georgian streets. **bathchristmasmarket.co.uk**
- St Nicholas Fair, York: another award-winning fair, this includes a festive fun fair and the Made in Yorkshire Yuletide Village. **visityork.org**
- Birmingham's Frankfurt Christmas Market: the biggest authentic German-style market outside Germany and Austria offers goodies ranging from pretzels, schnitzels, bratwursts and roasted almonds to glühwein, weissbeer (wheat beer), and hot chocolate. There's also live music and a neighbouring craft market. **thebfcm.co.uk**
- Winter Wonderland Nottingham: market stalls, entertainment, food and drink and ice-skating come together at the largest event in the East Midlands. **nottinghamwinterwonderland.co.uk**
- Manchester Christmas Markets: with more than 300 beautifully festooned stalls and chalets spread across the city centre, this trail of markets offers mouth-watering international food, drink and delicately crafted Yuletide gifts. **visitmanchester.com**
- Winchester Cathedral Christmas Market: widely regarded as one of Europe's best, this market sees more than 100 hand-picked exhibitors offering exclusive gifts that you won't find on the high street. **winchester-cathedral.org.uk**

lumiere-festival.com; longleat.co.uk; kew.org; canarywharf.com; forestryengland.uk; english-heritage.org.uk

ST CLEMENT'S DAY BLACKSMITHS' DEMONSTRATION

St Clement's Day is on 23 November and each year, on a nearby Saturday, members of the Worshipful Company and Guild of Blacksmiths (St Clement is their patron saint) gather at Finch Foundry, the last working water-powered forge in England, to demonstrate their craft. It all starts with a hearty "Blacksmith's breakfast", followed by a competition to make a particular piece of iron work in a set time, and includes the Snail Race, in which participants create a small iron snail as quickly as possible. Visitors will also be able to see the firing of the anvil, in which black powder is detonated on top to test it for strength. **nationaltrust.org.uk/finch-foundry**

CHRISTMAS TREE-THROWING

Have you ever wondered how far you can throw a six-foot Christmas tree? Well, wonder no more and enter this unusual event held each November in aid of charity. Entrants will be judged on the height as well as length of their throws over a carefully mapped course. You know you want to . . . **Keele Christmas Tree Farm, Newcastle-under-Lyme, Staffordshire. keelechristmastreefarm.co.uk**

DECEMBER 2021

ST NICHOLAS NIGHT

Every 6 December this community event marks the feast day of St Nicholas, the 4th-century bishop after whom the parish church in the town of Alcester is named. As well as a parade of the Boy Bishop and attendants (played by local children), and classic vehicles, there's shopping, rides, bands, Santa's grotto, and fireworks.
Alcester, Warwickshire. stnicholasnight.org

GRASSINGTON DICKENSIAN FESTIVAL

Transport yourself back to the time of Dickens in the picturesque village of Grassington in the Yorkshire Dales. Over two weekends in December there'll be shopkeepers, villagers and visitors dressed in Victorian costume, accompanied by bands, buskers and Victorian-style street entertainers, plus a traditional Christmas market, a Santa's grotto and a torch-lit nativity procession.
Grassington, North Yorkshire. grassingtondickensian.co.uk

SANTA DASH

If you can run, walk or drive a sleigh for 5k then why not join in with a fun, fancy-dress "Santa dash" this December? One of the largest is at Victoria Park in the heart of East London, which transforms into a festive course for thousands of runners dressed as Santa to spread cheer and raise money for charity. Places are limited, so claim yours early.
Victoria Park, London. londonsantarun.co.uk or santadash.co.uk for a list of others

TREE DRESSING

Taking place during National Tree Week at the Weald & Downland Living Museum, this ancient custom celebrates the life-giving properties of trees. Enjoy traditional songs, dances and plays with roots in the Green Man legends. Activities such as making a greenery headdress and jam-jar lantern are followed by a spiral dance around the aspen trees at dusk, and mulled apple juice.
Weald & Downland Living Museum, Singleton, Chichester, West Sussex. wealddown.co.uk

MONTOL

This six-day festival celebrates the solstice and Cornish midwinter traditions. After lantern and mask-making workshops, carol services, storytelling, plays and late-night shopping, the Festival culminates in Montol Eve on 21 December; starting with family-friendly activities during the day, followed by an edgier, adult menu of misrule. The main draw is a lantern-lit parade, with fire performers and 'Obby 'Osses, plus participants in formal wear and masks taking part in Guise dancing. It all ends in a grand street party.
Penzance, Cornwall. montolfestival.co.uk

CHASE THE PUDDING

Competitors and teams chase a man dressed as a Christmas pudding along a 5km beachfront route in Weymouth. It's all for charity of course, the Will Mackaness Trust which gives water sports opportunities to the young in Weymouth and Portland.
Weymouth, Dorset. willmackanesstrust.org.uk

Santas give chase on Weymouth Beach

MISTLETOE FESTIVAL AND AUCTION

Although the plant has been sold at various auctions around the country for hundreds of years, Tenbury Wells remains the last place steeped in mistletoe, as reported in the pages of *This England*, Winter 2019. The Mistletoe and Holly auction boasts some 500-1,500 lots and is held both on the last Tuesday in November and the first Tuesday in December at Burford House Garden Stores near Tenbury Wells. In recent years this has led to a mistletoe festival in Tenbury Wells on the first Saturday of December. Market and Craft stalls, a procession, Mistletoe Maidens and Holly Henchmen all feature in the day of celebration.
Tenbury Wells, Worcestershire. tenbury-mistletoe-festival.co.uk

Tenbury Mistletoe Festive Auction

WINTER WATCH AND SATURNALIA PARADE

Out on the streets of Chester, this midwinter spectacle features a re-enactment of the Winter Watch, a ceremony dating from the 15th century when the burghers would put the keys to the city in the safe hands of an early version of the local police force. The party really starts when the Lord of Misrule and a mischievous gathering including ice queens and even bloodthirsty cooks (bearing a head on a platter, no less) dance around the city centre to the beating of drums, with a finale of fire-breathing.
Chester, Cheshire. midsummerwatch.co.uk/winter-watch-parade

FESTIVE SWIMS

There's no better way to blow away those midwinter cobwebs than a bracing (some might say freezing) sea swim. They take place the length and breadth of the country on Christmas Day, Boxing Day and New Year's Day, with charity fund-raising the name of the game. You can run, walk or scream your way into the water from a beach, harbour, quayside, pier, weir or estuary, while a few festive dips even take place in lidos – though if they're heated we say that's cheating. Some winter dips strictly ban the wearing of wet suits, while others encourage elaborate fancy dress. The Seaburn Boxing Day dip, which started in 1974, claims to be the biggest of its kind in the northern hemisphere, attracting 1,000 swimmers and more than 5,000 supporters. It's time to rip off that Christmas jumper and freeze your baubles off . . .
outdoorswimmingsociety.com

More than 200 participants brave the cold water at Southend-on-Sea for the RNLI Boxing Day Dip

TOM BAWCOCK'S EVE

On the day before Christmas Eve villagers in Mousehole celebrate the heroic efforts of legendary Tom Bawcock, who is said to have alleviated a famine by going out to fish in a severe storm. Watch the lantern procession, enjoy the village's famous display of lights, then head to The Ship Inn and you'll be served a slice of stargazy pie, a fish pie with the heads sticking out of the pastry. The custom was the inspiration behind Antonia Barber's children's book *The Mousehole Cat.*
Mousehole, Cornwall.
shipinnmousehole.co.uk

BOXING DAY "SQUIRT"

While most of us are recovering from an over-indulgence of turkey and Christmas pudding, members of Geddington's volunteer fire brigade are busy with their annual Boxing Day "Squirt" – a water fight against rivals Kettering fire station – in which a beer barrel is suspended from a rope over the local river and two teams attempt to push the barrel over the heads of their opposition using hose jets. Visitors are advised to wear waterproof clothing . . .
Geddington, Northamptonshire.
gvfb.org/squirt

PAGHAM PRAM RACE

Set up by a group of demobbed servicemen in 1946 who decided they'd like a race over the Christmas period, one man would push the pram, another would sit in it. They'd have a pint of beer at every pub and the winner would be the recipient of a fruit cake. The prams have raced through the streets every year since, raising thousands of pounds for charity. There are now up to 60 entrants, and fancy-dress is rife. Rules are strict: the start is at 11 am prompt and the course is 3.3 miles long.
Pagham, West Sussex,
paghampramrace.com

MATLOCK BATH RAFT EVENT

Raising money for the RNLI, this Boxing Day "race" for decorated rafts attracts fearless, water-loving and slightly bonkers entrants from all over the country, who float along the River Derwent from Cawdor Quarry in Matlock to Cromford Meadows, watched by a huge turnout of spectators.
Matlock, Derbyshire.
matlockraftevent.co.uk

ALLENDALE TAR BAR'L

It's possible this spectacular New Year's Eve fire festival in the town of Allendale began as far back as the Middle Ages; it has been celebrated for at least 160 years. The focal point is a procession of 45 guisers – local men who carry whisky barrels filled with burning tar. At midnight they light a bonfire, as everyone shouts, "Be damned to he who throws last!" Wear warm clothes that won't ignite if a spark falls on them!
Allendale, Northumberland

NEW YEAR'S EVE FIREWORKS

They'll be happening all over the country, but the biggest event is in the capital, where the UK's largest annual fireworks display takes place over the London Eye to the accompaniment of Big Ben's "bongs". Bear in mind that, if you want to brave the crowds, you'll need a ticket to attend.
london.gov.uk

New Year Celebrations In London

Images: Shutterstock, Getty, Alamy

BEAUTIFUL TOWN
RYE

Rye in winter

Rye's fishing harbour on the River Rother

Mermaid Street in the old town

Gibbet Windmill which is a B&B

FOR those fascinated by the turbulent course of British history, a visit to the picturesque East Sussex port town of Rye is a must to discover more about the key defensive roles it played across various chapters of war and upheaval. Rising up from the surrounding, low-lying wetlands that lead out to the English Channel, the town's hilltop and fortified position made it ideally located to protect the south coast from a variety of marauders. In the second half of the 12th-century Rye became a limb town of the prestigious Cinque Ports, a confederation of south-coast defensive towns.

Today, the town's story is recounted in two museum sites, one housed in the 13th-century Ypres Tower, built to repel French invasion attempts, and the East Street Museum, found within a former bottling factory. Exhibitions showcase examples of the town's celebrated pottery and wooden Tunbridge ware, and artefacts such as the gruesome gibbet and skull of notorious 18th-century murderer John Breads. There's also a model of the changing Romney Marsh coastline and a smuggler's lantern that hints at the illicit activities of past residents.

Rye's charming network of sloping and cobbled streets and alleyways offers architectural styles – from half-timbered medieval to Georgian houses – that are as diverse as its many shops and eateries. Wander through countless trendy fashion stores, antiques and artisan shops and art galleries. Visit the UK's largest collection of working antique end-of-the-pier games at Rye Heritage Centre, or treat yourself with a visit to *Antiques Roadshow* glass expert Andy McConnell's Glass Etc, the country's largest collection of antique and 20th-century glass, or seek out a keepsake from Rye Pottery's range of handmade English ceramics. For something entirely different and close to the railway station, Alex MacArthur Interiors offers viewings, by appointment only, of her ancient monastery that's stuffed with stunning antiques and architectural pieces.

Then there is the mouth-watering menu of independent cafés, cosy historic pubs and cutting-edge restaurants throughout the town. Those worth a visit include the "sheep-shack chic" of The Globe Inn Marsh, the classic style of The George in Rye, and Webbe's for local, seasonal seafood.

Nature lovers can walk off lunch and escape the crowds at the Rye Harbour Nature Reserve. The reserve's miles of accessible footpaths take in the beautiful mixed habitat of shingle, grassland, saltmarsh and reedbeds that is home to over 4,500 species of plants and animals.

Each year, the bustling town hosts a packed calendar of events including the Rye International Jazz and Blues Festival in August, the Rye Festival of the Sea and the fortnight-long Rye Festival of Art, both in September.

RICHARD GINGER

DON'T MISS

Lamb House

Built in 1723 by wine merchant and politician James Lamb, this Georgian property has provided accommodation for a host of historic and literary luminaries, including King George I in 1726. Its most famous former resident is author Henry James who wrote the novella *The Turn of the Screw*, and novels *The Wings of the Dove* and *The Ambassadors*. The house has a collection of James's memorabilia.
nationaltrust.org.uk/lamb-house

Rye Heritage Centre

Discover the story of Rye and places to visit in the town here. However, the main attraction is the Rye Town Model Show, built by hand by Joy and Ted Harland. Joy crafted the 1:100 scale model by drawing from written records, building surveys, aerial photographs and a 19th-century map. Ted wired lights and created the audio track, bringing 700 years of history to life.
ryeheritage.co.uk

The Parish Church of St Mary

For over 900 years St Mary's has dominated Rye's skyline. In 1561-2 a clock was installed in the church tower and remains in good order to this day. Visitors can climb the tower to enjoy views of the countryside and admire the church's 18th-century bells that have a combined weight of almost five tons.
ryeparishchurch.org.uk

Images: Shutterstock, Alamy

WORDS OF POWER

Simon Sebag Montefiore presents four of England's finest orators, examining what makes their words so powerful and lasting

IN an orator, the acuteness of the logicians, the wisdom of the philosophers, the language almost of poetry, the memory of lawyers, the voice of tragedians, the gesture almost of the best actors, is required. Nothing therefore is more rarely found among mankind than a consummate orator." So wrote Cicero, one of Rome's finest public speakers, in his essay *On Oratory.* "It was written in 55 BC but is just as true today," says historian and author Simon Sebag Montefiore.

Here, Simon presents four great orators from his recently published book *Voices of History: Speeches that Changed the World*, revealing the key to their brilliance.

TIMELESSNESS: OLIVER CROMWELL

Many of these speeches are as viscerally relevant today even though they were delivered centuries ago. In the age of populism, Brexit and Trumpism, when widespread indignation and exasperation with traditional parliaments and professional politicians is fierce, Cromwell's furious attack on his own parliamentarians [here] sounds familiar to us. He felt he was "draining the swamp" . . . [though] never has political exasperation been expressed with such irascible intemperance as this speech in his dismissal of an obstructive Parliament. Cromwell ruled Britain as Lord Protector from 1653 until his death in 1658.

Oliver Cromwell by Robert Walker, circa 1649

"IN THE NAME OF GOD, GO!"
20 APRIL, 1653

It is high time for me to put an end to your sitting in this place, which you have dishonoured by your contempt of all virtue, and defiled by your practice of every vice; ye are a factious crew, and enemies to all good government; ye are a pack of mercenary wretches, and would like Esau sell your country for a mess of potage, and like Judas betray your God for a few pieces of money; is there a single virtue now remaining amongst you? Is there one vice you do not possess? Ye have no more religion than my horse; gold is your God; which of you have not barter'd your conscience for bribes? Is there a man amongst you that has the least care for the good of the Commonwealth? Ye sordid prostitutes have you not defil'd this sacred place, and turn'd the Lord's temple into a den of thieves, by your immoral principles and wicked practices? Ye are grown intolerably odious to the whole nation; you were deputed here by the people to get grievances redress'd, are yourselves become the greatest grievance. Your country therefore calls upon me to cleanse this Augean stable, by putting a final period to your iniquitous proceedings in this House; and which by God's help, and the strength he has given me, I am now come to do; I command ye therefore, upon the peril of your lives, to depart immediately out of this place; go, get you out! Make haste! Ye venal slaves be gone! Go! Take away that shining bauble there, and lock up the doors. In the name of God, go!

DEFIANCE: ELIZABETH I

Portrait of Queen Elizabeth I, circa 1550-99

In 1588, Philip II of Spain decided to send an Armada of 130 ships bearing 18,000 soldiers to invade England. It set sail, to link up with a further 30,000 men in the Spanish Netherlands. Elizabeth faced panic on all sides as she mustered an army – more of a makeshift militia – at Tilbury and deployed the fleet in the Channel under Admirals Lord Howard of Effingham and Drake. On 28 and 29 July her admirals sent in fireships that destroyed many Spanish ships and forced others out to sea. Little of the Armada returned to Spain.

Elizabeth I inspects her troops at Tilbury, 1588

However, before the news reached Elizabeth, she inspected the army, and gave this speech. Her command of English, as seen in her many letters and speeches, is masterful.

"THE HEART AND STOMACH OF A KING"
8 AUGUST, 1588

My loving people,

We have been persuaded by some that are careful of our safety, to take heed how we commit ourselves to armed multitudes, for fear of treachery; but I assure you I do not desire to live to distrust my faithful and loving people. Let tyrants fear, I have always so behaved myself that, under God, I have placed my chiefest strength and safeguard in the loyal hearts and good-will of my subjects; and therefore I am come amongst you, as you see, at this time, not for my recreation and disport, but being resolved, in the midst and heat of the battle, to live and die amongst you all; to lay down for my God, and for my kingdom, and my people, my honour and my blood, even in the dust. I know I have the body but of a weak and feeble woman; but I have the heart and stomach of a king, and of a king of England too, and think foul scorn that Parma or Spain, or any prince of Europe, should dare to invade the borders of my realm; to which rather than any dishonour shall grow by me, I myself will take up arms, I myself will be your general, judge, and rewarder of every one of your virtues in the field. I know already, for your forwardness you have deserved rewards and crowns; and We do assure you in the word of a prince, they shall be duly paid you. In the meantime, my lieutenant general shall be in my stead, than whom never prince commanded a more noble or worthy subject; not doubting but by your obedience to my general, by your concord in the camp, and your valour in the field, we shall shortly have a famous victory over those enemies of my God, of my kingdom, and of my people.

Queen Elizabeth delivers her speech at Tilbury

PASSION: EMMELINE PANKHURST

Emmeline Pankhurst in Boston, 1910

"Freedom or death" was the choice posed by Pankhurst, the leader of the Suffragette movement that campaigned for women's right to vote at the turn of the 20th century . . . From throwing axes at the Prime Minister to breaking the windows in Downing Street and fighting with police, the struggle intensified. When she was in prison, Pankhurst led hunger strikes to which the authorities reacted by the horrendous trauma of forced feeding to keep the suffragettes alive.

Emmeline Pankhurst on the campaign trail

Introducing herself as a "hooligan", Pankhurst made her first visit to the US in 1909 and in 1913, released from jail, she returned to America to give this speech.

"I AM HERE AS A SOLDIER"
13 NOVEMBER, 1913

I do not come here as an advocate, because whatever position the suffrage movement may occupy in the United States of America, in England it has passed beyond the realm of advocacy and it has entered into the sphere of practical politics. It has become the subject of revolution and civil war, and so tonight I am not here to advocate woman suffrage. American suffragists can do that very well for themselves.

I am here as a soldier who has temporarily left the field of battle in order to explain – it seems strange it should have to be explained – what civil war is like when civil war is waged by women . . . If I were a man and I said to you, "I come from a country which professes to have representative institutions and yet denies me, a taxpayer, an inhabitant of the country, representative rights," you would at once understand that that human being, being a man, was justified in the adoption of revolutionary methods to get representative institutions. But since I am a woman it is necessary in the twentieth century to explain why women have adopted revolutionary methods in order to win the rights of citizenship . . . Now, I want to say to you who think women cannot succeed, we have brought the government of England to this position, that it has to face this alternative: either women are to be killed or women are to have the vote.

I ask American men in this meeting, what would you say if in your State you were faced with that alternative, that you must either kill them or give them their citizenship – women, many of whom you respect, women whom you know have lived useful lives, women whom you know, even if you do not know them personally, are animated with the highest motives, women who are in pursuit of liberty and the power to do useful public service? Well, there is only one answer to that alternative; there is only one way out of it, unless you are prepared to put back civilization two or three generations: you must give those women the vote. Now that is the outcome of our civil war.

Emmeline Pankhurst being arrested outside Buckingham Palace, 1914

Churchill making a speech outside the Conservative Club, Wanstead, and posing with their mascot bulldog

"All great speakers were bad speakers at first," argued American essayist [Ralph Waldo] Emerson. This is not always true: [Georges] Danton was a born speaker – you can hear his passionate energy. [But] Churchill, who started with a slight stammer and a lisp, proves Emerson's point. He wrote his speeches by hand, over and over again, correcting and polishing. Hitler's performances were theatrical spectaculars of physical athleticism, sometimes lasting hours, delivered to crowds first in sweaty beer halls then in illuminated stadiums. Yet on paper, his phrases seem mediocre. Churchill's were the opposite, delivered stolidly in the House of Commons or BBC studio, but the phrases are golden and timeless.

The Germans rolled through Belgium and Holland and into France, trapping the British Army at Dunkirk. Faced with the downfall of the great land power of France, Churchill knew only the Channel stood between Nazi Panzers and a lightly defended Britain [when he made this speech].

"WE SHALL FIGHT ON THE BEACHES"
4 JUNE, 1940

I have, myself, full confidence that if all do their duty, if nothing is neglected, and if best arrangements are made, as they are being made, we shall prove ourselves once again able to defend our island home, to ride out the storm of war, and to outlive the menace of tyranny, if necessary for years, if necessary alone. At any rate, that is what we are going to try to do. That is the resolve of His Majesty's government – every man of them. That is the will of Parliament and the nation. The British Empire and the French Republic, linked together in their cause and in their need, will defend to the death their native soil, aiding each other like good comrades to the utmost of their strength.

Even though large tracts of Europe and many old and famous states have fallen or may fall into the grip of the Gestapo and all the odious apparatus of Nazi rule, we shall not flag or fail. We shall go on to the end, we shall fight in France, we shall fight on the seas and oceans, we shall fight with growing confidence and growing strength in the air, we shall defend our island, whatever the cost may be, we shall fight on the beaches, we shall fight on the landing grounds, we shall fight in the fields and in the streets, we shall fight in the hills; we shall never surrender, and even if, which I do not for a moment believe, this island or a large part of it were subjugated and starving, then our empire beyond the seas, armed and guarded by the British fleet, would carry on the struggle, until, in God's good time, the New World, with all its power and might, steps forth to the rescue and the liberation of the old.

Churchill addressing the nation

A celebration of, and warning against, the power of words, *Voices of History: Speeches that Changed the World* presents more than 70 speeches from the inspiring to the most despicable. *Simon Sebag Montefiore. Orion Publishing; £14.99*

Images: Shutterstock, Alamy

IT'S ALL IN THE NAME

From Eton Mess to Bury Black Pudding, Olivia Greenway discovers the origins of our favourite foods

THE majority of people living in the Middle Ages and up to the Industrial Revolution worked in the countryside and were uneducated. So the recipes that proved popular and were made regularly would be passed on from a mother to her daughters down through the generations.

Produce was seasonal, with usually a surplus in summer and a shortage in winter. With no refrigeration, eggs, milk and butter would have to be used in recipes to prevent spoilage. Until the advent of the railways, from the mid 19th century on, travel was difficult and expensive. Most people stayed around their home, perhaps only venturing to a summer fair to buy and trade once a year, so recipes remained regional. Often it was local circumstances that determined the foodstuff; other times it was down to individual creativity or serendipity.

Images: Getty, Shutterstock and Alamy

Melton Mowbray Pork Pie

Waste (whey) from cheese-making in Leicestershire was in ample supply for pig food, so relatively cheap pork meat was chopped, made into a pie and eaten cold out in the fields.

Using hot water crust pastry, the Melton Mowbray pie is baked loose on a tray. This results in a slightly bowed out shape. The pork meat is always chopped, and natural bone stock jelly added when the pie has cooled. It solidifies and then helps to keep the pie moist. The Melton Mowbray pork pie was granted PGI (Protected Geographical Indication) status in 2009. This means it has to be made within a certain area. Authentic pies are made from uncured pork with a high meat content.

Mary Dickinson, who died in 1841, made the first pork pies. Ten years later, her grandson opened his pork pie shop, using her recipe.

Where to buy: *Dickinson & Morris, Nottingham Street, Melton Mowbray LE13 1NW. porkpie.co.uk*

Eton Mess

Tradition has it that this popular dessert was first made at the famous English public school. But why? One account suggests a pavlova was knocked over by a Labrador on the loose, and the results were scooped up and served in individual bowls. However, pavlova was named after the Russian ballet dancer Anna Pavlova – the meringue representing her tutu – and the Eton Mess predates this period. The first record of the name Eton Mess in print was in 1893. It was

Melton Mowbray Pork Pie

Eton Mess

Kendal Mint Cake

said to have been first served at the annual cricket match between Eton and rival school Harrow. Former Tory minister William Waldegrave argues that Eton Mess doesn't exist and should be called Strawberry Mess. Wherever it comes from, it's a delicious, easy to prepare dish.

Kendal Mint Cake

My biggest disappointment as a teenager was to discover that Kendal Mint Cake is not a cake at all, but a peppermint slab. Once I had a nibble of the imposter, however, I was hooked. The recipe is said to have been discovered by accident. Boiling sugar, intended to make sticks of rock, was mistakenly left on overnight and the mixture turned opaque.

The precise recipe is secret, but it involves boiling water with sugar and stirring to give the mixture its characteristic cloudy quality. Then peppermint oil is added before the mixture is poured into moulds and cooled. It's enjoyed by hikers and outdoor sports enthusiasts who need an energy boost. Edmund Hillary took mint cake on his ascent of Mount Everest in 1953.

Where to buy: *Quiggin's claims to be the oldest supplier, established in 1870 in Kendal. originalkendalmintcake.co.uk*

Maid of Honour Tarts

These tarts date back to Tudor times. Henry VIII observed the queen's maids enjoying some pastries. Intrigued, he ordered some to be made for him, and declared they should be baked regularly. The tart has a flaky pastry base and is filled with sweet curd cheese. Henry named them Maid of Honour tarts. It is said he kept the recipe to himself, but in the 18th century, the Original Maids of Honour tea room was set up and still exists, not far from Hampton Court Palace.

Where to buy: *Newens, The Original Maids of Honour, 288 Kew Road, Kew Gardens, Richmond-upon-Thames TW9 3DU. theoriginalmaidsofhonour.co.uk*

Sticky Toffee Pudding

It's hard to imagine a world without sticky toffee pudding, so popular is it on British menus. However, it was only invented in the 1970s. Sharrow Bay Hotel was one of the first country house hotels in the UK and it was here that owner Francis Coulson developed his date-filled sponge recipe, smothered in a rich toffee sauce. There are many imitations, but to taste the best you have to dine there. Their recipe is a closely guarded secret; staff have to sign a non-disclosure agreement!

Where to buy: *Cartmel sticky toffee pudding has been made in small batches for 20 years. It can be bought in Fortnum and Mason, Waitrose, Booths, farm shops and online. cartmelvillageshop.co.uk*

Bakewell Pudding

This pudding is not well known outside Derbyshire, where it originated. Legend has it that, once again, the pudding was the result of a mistake. Around 1820, the cook from the White Horse Inn left written instructions for her assistant to make a jam tart. Probably her assistant could not read; in any case she got the recipe wrong, but the result was so delicious, the Bakewell pudding became a regular on the menu. A flaky pastry base is covered with jam, and then a mixture of eggs, butter and ground almonds are spread on top and baked. A variation – Bakewell tart – is a more modern interpretation which has an icing sugar topping.

Where to buy: *buy in-store, learn to make it, or order online. bakewellpuddingshop.co.uk*

Cumberland Sausage

It's said the Cumberland sausage has been made in the area for over 500 years. Now part of Cumbria, during the 18th century the port of Whitehaven used to import spices from the West Indies. Black and white pepper and nutmeg worked well in flavouring the sausage. In 2011, the Cumberland sausage was awarded PGI status and sausages with this accreditation have to be made in Cumbria from at least 80% meat and sold in a long coil.

Where to buy: *Sillfield Farm,* >

Sticky Toffee Pudding

Eccles Cakes

> *in Barrow-in-Furness, Cumbria, sells PGI Cumberland sausages made from their own free-range pigs at the local market and online. sillfield.co.uk*

Eccles Cakes

Known by local children as "squashed fly cakes", these pastries originated in Eccles, now part of Manchester. It's not known who invented the recipe, but the first known commercial outlet was opened in Salford town centre in 1793. The pastries are individual round cakes made with flaky pastry and butter, and filled with currants. Currants are a variety of black dried grapes and slightly tart in flavour. Nowadays, the finished item is sometimes dusted with caster sugar.

Where to buy: *Real Lancashire Eccles cakes are handmade and the most well-known brand. The company has been making them to a family recipe since 1979. Available in most supermarkets, they are sold in packs of four.*

Coventry Godcakes

Unsurprisingly, Godcakes have a religious connection. These triangular puff pastry tarts, filled with mincemeat and sprinkled with sugar, have three slashes on the top said to represent the Holy Trinity. In Coventry, they are given by godparents to their godchildren in the New Year. Godcakes have been produced in the city since the Middle Ages, but the practice died out with the last bakery that made them. That is, until they were revived in 2008 by a local guide, and keen home baker. Unfortunately, despite the business's success, the effect of the coronavirus on trading conditions caused it to close in March 2020.

Parkin

Parkin is a ginger cake from the north of England, dating back to the Middle Ages. The key ingredients are black treacle and oats. Black treacle is a by-product of sugar refining, and became increasingly common from the 16th century. Parkin keeps well – it has no eggs – and tastes even better if it's been matured for a while, as it gets sticky and the flavours intensify. The cake is associated with Guy Fawkes Night, as this is when the first oat harvest is expected, and fresh oats make the best parkin. It was originally cooked over an open fire and made at home.

Where to buy: *Lottie Shaw carries on a baking tradition started by her aunts in Yorkshire a century ago. Her parkin won a Great Taste award in 2018. lottieshaws.co.uk*

Bury Black Pudding

Black pudding is a type of early sausage made using animal blood. It is associated with the Black Country and north-west England, especially Bury, where it is still sold in the famous open-air market. Fat and rusk are added to the pork blood, along with spices and local herbs such as pennyroyal, which has a slight minty flavour. Beef intestines would be filled with this mixture and then boiled. Black pudding is best sliced and fried to complement a full English breakfast. It is an excellent source of protein and high in zinc and iron.

Where to buy: *Bury Black Pudding Company products can be bought at major supermarkets and online. They also make a vegetarian and vegan version. buryblackpuddings.co.uk*

Grasmere Gingerbread

Grasmere gingerbread – like a thick biscuit or shortbread – is baked daily and sold in a 17th-century former school that was once the home of the original maker of the gingerbread, Sarah Nelson. Sited next to St Oswald's Church (where William Wordsworth is buried), the tiny premises can only hold a few people at a time. In keeping with its Victorian origins, staff wear dress from the period. The gingerbread keeps for about a week, but it's hard to resist eating on the spot!

Where to buy: *The gingerbread is made to a secret recipe (said to be kept in a bank vault in the village) and only available at the shop, or online. Church Cottage, Grasmere, Ambleside LA22 9SW. grasmeregingerbread.co.uk*

Coventry Godcakes

Parkin

Bury Black Pudding

A FESTIVE FINALE

Food writer Angela Romeo celebrates the brilliant, if button-popping, Christmas Pudding . . .

THERE are not many desserts that can land on the table with a little thud and a roaring flame and be met with genuine joy, merriment *and* a round of applause! Steeped in history (and alcohol), it's no wonder that the Christmas pudding has survived hundreds of years as a must-have on our festive menu.

Strangely, this festive stalwart is believed to have begun life as savoury "frumenty" or "pottage" – both porridge-like stews made of beef and mutton with dried fruit, wine and spices. It became a festive staple in the Middle Ages, taking on the name "plum pottage". Back then, the word "plum" referred to any dried fruit.

As preserving techniques for meat improved in the 18th-century, the savoury element diminished. People started to add sugar and more fruit and the dish was increasingly referred to as "plum pudding". A popular myth from this period says that the 13 ingredients traditionally used in this festive treat represent Christ's 13 disciples. The mixture would be stirred east to west to honour the Three Wise Men and their journey.

One of the earliest recipes for plum pudding was written by Mary Kettilby in her 1714 book, *A Collection of Above Three Hundred Receipts in Cookery, Physick and Surgery*. It's a simple recipe for "Plumb-Pudding", made using only shredded suet, raisins, flour, sugar, eggs and a little salt. "Tie it up in clofe, and boil it four hours at least," she stipulates. With six ingredients and a snappy method, clearly Mary wasn't one for tradition.

Shutterstock

Plum pudding did have a little blip from festive favour with Oliver Cromwell in the 17th-century. He banned it, along with all festive celebrations, in an attempt to tackle festive gluttony. When King Charles II came to power, Christmas was restored and the pud firmly back on our plates.

A tradition that remains in many households is making your pudding on last Sunday before Advent – known as Stir-up Sunday as the collect of the day begins "Stir up, we beseech thee, O Lord, the wills of thy faithful people" – recognised as the last day to make your pudding. The whole family can get involved with stirring and make a wish.

Of course, the tradition of adding a silver sixpence to the mix isn't to be forgotten, and wouldn't be if you were the "lucky" one to bite down on it! It is said to bring the finder a year of good luck.

As with lots of traditions, it's the Victorian era that closely matches how we treat the Christmas pudding today. Charles Dickens describes the moment in *A Christmas Carol*: "In half a minute Mrs Cratchit entered – flushed, but smiling proudly – with the pudding, like a speckled cannon-ball, so hard and firm, blazing in half-a-quartern of ignited brandy, and bedight with Christmas holly stuck into the top."

Even the sprig of holly has grounds for its placement. It looks wonderfully festive, but its said to represent the crown of thorns.

So are other puds going to knock our festive favourite off its seasonal top spot? Mulled wine sorbet? Mince-pie ice-cream? Yule log? One thing to be sure of is if these bright gems end up on the table, this flaming dark beauty will follow. There's *always* room for Christmas pudding . . . and time for a lie down afterwards!

HOW TO FLAME A CHRISTMAS PUDDING

1) Turn the steamed Christmas pudding out on to a serving plate with a good-sized rim.

2) Pour 2-3 tbsp of brandy, dark rum or whisky into a long-handled metal-based ladle.

3) Holding the ladle carefully, heat the spirit over a gas hob ring until the spirit is really hot (if you don't have a gas stove, heat in a small saucepan first then transfer to a ladle).

4) Tilt the ladle slightly into the gas flame to ignite, or use a long-handled kitchen lighter.

5) Once alight, immediately pour over the Christmas pudding. Make sure the flames have gone out before cutting into portions and serving.

The Blue Dining Room at Waddesdon Manor

Peter Greenway/National Trust

A mantelpiece at Holkham Hall

The main entrance hall at Castle Howard

On a journey at Chatsworth House

DECK THE (HISTORIC) HALLS

If you'd like a lesson in how to decorate for Christmas, look no further than England's finest stately homes, says Katherine Sorrell

>

The decorated mantelpiece in the Blue Dining Room at Waddesdon

Stars burst from the ceiling at Waddesdon

Holkham Hall courtyard dressed with many illuminated trees

IF you like to get your Christmas tree in place early, you're in excellent company! The Queen's Nordmann fir at Windsor Castle is usually set up from around the end of November in St George's Hall, where it dazzles with thousands of lights and ornaments. At more than 20 feet high, it almost sweeps the vaulted ceiling of this impressive neo-Gothic room, and reputedly takes a day and a half to decorate, with teams of staff using very tall ladders indeed.

Christmas finery makes the already sumptuous castle absolutely sublime – as befits the place where Queen Victoria and Prince Albert spent every one of their 20 Christmases together. Additional trees, garlands and lights adorn other areas of the state apartments and semi-state rooms, while the table in the State Dining Room is laid with silver-gilt pieces from the spectacular Grand Service, which was commissioned by George IV and is still used today by the Queen and her guests at state banquets.

At many other stately homes around the country, the festive decorations are similarly extravagant – as one would expect in destinations that were built to impress and entertain. Visitors to our most beautiful and iconic houses will find awe-inspiring festive adornments both inside and out, from enormous trees to illuminated trails, as well as a range of attractions and events to celebrate the season.

Seemingly no expense is spared in the effort to delight visitors, although, as James Probert of Historic Houses points out, these are mostly lived-in homes, so while the mansions, manors and castles might get dressed up to the nines, they are also a welcoming family house to enjoy personal celebrations.

"From illuminated trails to glorious traditional decorations, choir performances to audiences with Father Christmas, or candlelit tours after dark, going to a historic house is the best way to get into the Christmas spirit," he says.

"There's a real heart to places where open fires are really lit, dogs sit on the furniture, and you might even encounter the owner putting up the last sprigs of holly round the next corner."

Highclere Castle, home to the

The magnificent tree in St George's Hall at Windsor Castle

Earl and Countess of Carnavon (and filming location of *Downton Abbey*), has a busy Christmas programme of tours and teas, carol singing and gift fairs. In the past, the castle has also hosted a special Christmas dinner, with champagne, canapés and a three-course dinner, followed by a guided tour of the grand reception rooms, and carol singing around the tree.

To decorate the house, holly and mistletoe are gathered from the grounds, and the centrepiece, as at Windsor, is a 20-foot tree, in this case a Norwegian Spruce, hung with white lights, baubles and small figures and then painstakingly hoisted into place. Lady Carnavon has written a book called *Christmas at Highclere*, a look behind the scenes at this magical time at one of the most famous houses in the world, and she adores the family's personal Christmas traditions, which include setting out a mince pie and a glass of Baileys for Santa by the fireplace, and eating leftover Christmas pudding fried in butter.

History really comes to the fore in many houses at Christmas. At the Tudor Paycocke's House and Garden in Essex, for example, there's a 16th-century theme, featuring re-enactment group the Companye of Merrie Folke, while Wimpole Hall in Cambridgeshire usually relives the decadent festivities of Georgian England, with hand-made decorations, stirring the plum pudding and a programme of Georgian Baroque music.

Coleton Fishacre and Castle Drogo, both in Devon, have featured 1920s themes. Croft Castle in Herefordshire has focused on the war years of the 1940s, and Hanbury Hall, Worcestershire, turned back the clock for some 1970s and 80s nostalgia, including Babycham, games and pop hits from Slade.

A large number of historic houses go all out with a handsome Victorian theme – it was, after all, the Victorians who created many of our Christmas traditions, from decorated trees to greetings cards, crackers to gift-giving, carols to the centrepiece of a roast turkey.

At Cotehele, Cornwall, for example, in 2019 the mill was opened at Christmas for a special "Victorian family Christmas", offering insights into the decorations and way of life of the Langford family who once lived >

Stuart Bebb/National Trust

Walking in a winter wonderland at Waddesdon Manor

CHRISTMAS AT TEN OF OUR GRANDEST STATELY HOMES

Bear in mind that many events are ticket-only and can sell out well in advance, so it pays to plan early

Blenheim

One of England's largest houses, Blenheim – the birthplace of Sir Winston Churchill – is a UNESCO World Heritage Site. At Christmas, its Baroque interiors are magnificently decorated to a different theme each year, and outside there's a Christmas market and a spectacular, mile-long Illuminated Trail through its world-famous parkland.
Woodstock, Oxfordshire OX20 1PP, 01993 810530; blenheimpalace.com

Castle Howard

This magnificent 18th-century house is one of the great palaces of Europe – and famous for its part in the film and TV series *Brideshead Revisited.* Elaborate decorations transform the house each festive season. Live music, twilight tours, an artisan market and visits to Santa are extra reasons to visit.
Castle Howard Estate, York YO60 7DA, 01653 648333; castlehoward.co.uk

Chatsworth

One of our finest examples of an English stately home, Chatsworth has been handed down through 16 generations of the Cavendish family. The house is famous for its festive displays, and also offers a Christmas market with more than 100 stalls.
Bakewell, Derbyshire DE45 1PP, 01246 565300; chatsworth.org

Cotehele

A Tudor house with medieval roots, Cotehele,

> there. Belton House in Lincolnshire has featured Victorian fairground rides, and visitors to Scotney Castle in Kent enjoyed roaring fires, the dining table laid ready for a Victorian feast, and beds hung with stockings.

Enormous time and effort goes into preparing for the festive period, which brings tens of thousands of additional people through the doors of these sometimes cash-strapped houses. Castle Howard in North Yorkshire, for example, welcomes more than 50,000 visitors each Christmas, and its design team consists of theatrical set designers, prop makers, florists and costume designers, supported by a small but devoted army of gardeners, building services and facilities crew. It takes them several weeks, working flat out, to dress every inch of the house for the festive season. And if the dozens of trees and tens of thousands of baubles and decorations were not enough, the house also offers entertainment, twilight tours, a huge artisan market and a resident Santa Claus.

At Chatsworth House, Derbyshire, planning for the next Christmas starts the moment the decorations are packed away. The festive weeks are the most important of its year, enjoyed by more than 100,000 visitors, and in 2019 a documentary crew from Channel Four followed the behind-the-scenes transformation as, in five days, housekeepers, designers, gardeners and foresters decorated the house with more than 30 Christmas trees, 60,000 baubles and a million fairy lights.

Its theme was "A Land Far, Far Away", while previous years' designs have taken influences from Charles Dickens, Russia, carols and children's stories.

perched above the River Tamar, was the ancestral home to the Edgcumbe family. Famous for its enormous dried-flower Christmas garland, Cotehele also offers other festive attractions, including musical performances and "A Victorian Christmas" at its mill.
St Dominick, near Saltash, Cornwall PL12 6TA, 01579 351346; nationaltrust.org.uk/cotehele

Haddon Hall

The 900-year-old house contains the most important early English furniture collection in England, and nationally important tapestries. For the festive season the hall is decked out with medieval decorations, and hosts candlelit tours, as well as a market and a programme of music and craft workshops.
Bakewell, Derbyshire DE45 1LA, 01629 812 855; haddonhall.co.uk

Harewood House

Expect an exciting Christmas theme at Harewood! Past events have included a lavish Victorian Christmas, a fantasy 1920s dreamscape and the house coming "alive". Also workshops, music, market weekends, cooking demonstrations and an opportunity to meet with Father and Mrs Christmas.
Harewood, Leeds LS17 9LG, 0113 218 1010; harewood.org

Highclere

Known as "the real Downton Abbey", the opulent, "Jacobethan"-style Highclere Castle is the home of the 8th Earl and Countess of Carnarvon. At Christmas, you can look forward to a magnificent tree, decorative themes based on the house's Victorian past, tours, teas, carol singing and gift fairs.
Highclere Park, Newbury, Berkshire RG20 9RN, 01635 253210; highclerecastle.co.uk

Holkham Hall

This 18th century Palladian-style house was built by Thomas Coke, 1st Earl of Leicester, and is still the home of the 8th Earl and his family. Enjoy candlelit tours of the magnificently decorated state rooms, craft masterclasses, a food fair, and meeting Father and Mother Christmas with their ukulele-playing elves.
Wells-next-the-Sea, Norfolk NR23 1AB, 01328 713111; holkham.co.uk

Waddesdon

A 19th-century French Renaissance-style château, filled with royal treasures and many objects with an exceptional story to tell. Christmas features include a Winter Light Trail, Christmas Fair, light show, festive walks and displays in the house.
Aylesbury, Buckinghamshire HP18 0JH, 01296 820414; waddesdon.org.uk

Windsor Castle

The oldest and largest occupied castle in the world, where the Queen spends most of her private weekends. Christmas highlights include not only the tree in St George's Hall and the Grand Service laid in the State Dining Room, but also pantomime performances, arts and crafts activities and days especially for families.
Windsor, Berkshire SL4 1NJ, 0303 123 7304; rct.uk/visit/windsor-castle

The state dining room at Windsor Castle

The decorative focus is not only on the gorgeous interiors of these grand properties. In many cases the grounds are embellished with lighting designs that are as much of an attraction as the house itself.

At Blenheim Palace in Oxfordshire, for example, a splendidly decorated interior – with a different theme each year – complements a superlative light trail through its festive gardens. The mile-long path winds its way through the world-famous parkland, featuring aerial light shows, glowing flowers, a laser garden, a scented fire garden, a tunnel of light and a finale of beams of light that dance across the historic façade, accompanied by Christmas music.

Waddesdon, the Rothschild house in Buckinghamshire, offers a similarly impressive exterior experience, with its distinctive architecture brought to life with coloured lighting and the sound of Christmas classics, while trees and bushes are draped in sparkle and a Winter Light Trail full of features such as floodlit disco balls and a cascading river of light. There's also a Christmas fair with more than 80 chalets selling artisan food and craft.

"Christmas is a magical time at Waddesdon," says Pippa Shirley, head of collections and gardens. "The great Rothschild traditions of hospitality and attention to detail are very much to the fore, from the welcome at the front door to the care and attention that the chefs put into making our own mincemeat. We love seeing families and children enjoying its unique atmosphere, sparkle, glamour and fun. The Manor looks like a fairy-tale castle at the best of times, so at Christmas it is truly enchanting."

QUIZ ANSWERS

GEOGRAPHY QUIZ ANSWERS FROM PAGE 25

1 Northumberland **2** Suffolk **3** Bristol
4 Swindon, Wiltshire **5** Crosby, Merseyside
6 Huntingdonshire and Cambridgeshire
7 Chichester, West Sussex
8 The Goyt and the Tame and they join in Stockport.
9 Yorkshire Dales National Park
10 East Sussex **11** Gateshead, 2002
12 The Lake District National Park **13** Derbyshire
14 Coventry **15** Norwich **16** West Sussex **17** Ipswich
18 Morpeth **19** Ross-on-Wye, Herefordshire
20 Bedfordshire **21** Buckinghamshire **22** Somerset
23 Leominster **24** Plymouth **25** Abbotsbury, Dorset
26 Cheltenham **27** Macclesfield **28** Cornwall
29 Somerset **30** Huntingdon **31** Southwold
32 Greensted, Essex **33** Margate, Kent
34 Hertfordshire **35** Devon
36 Chawton, Hampshire **37** York **38** River Lune
39 Dungeness, Kent **40** Bury St Edmunds
41 Bridgnorth **42** Buckinghamshire
43 Chatham, Kent **44** North York Moors National Park **45** Cumbria **46** Sandwich, Kent
47 1890, Hampshire **48** Swanage **49** Lyme Regis
50 Newlyn Bay

GREAT BRITISH FILM QUIZ ANSWERS FROM PAGE 76

1 King George VI **2** Gilbert and Sullivan **3** Deborah Kerr **4** *Goodbye, Mr Chips* **5** Noël Coward **6** Olivia Colman **7** *Passport to Pimlico* **8** A steel-rimmed bowler hat **9** Anthony Minghella **10** Moira Shearer **11** *Brighton Rock* **12** *The Prime of Miss Jean Brodie* **13** Timothy Spall **14** Anthony Burgess **15** Robert Donat **16** William Thomas Wells, better known as Bombardier Billy Wells **17** *Oliver!* **18** Sally Anne Howes **19** Bob Hoskins **20** *Women in Love* **21** Hammer **22** *My Cousin Rachel* **23** Edward Woodward **24** *Kind Hearts and Coronets*. **25** Peter Greenaway **26** *Get Carter* **27** Henry V **28** Carol Reed **29** *A Matter of Life and Death* **30** Mick Jagger **31***The Bridge on the River Kwai* **32** Amanda Barrie **33** Peter Sellers as Inspector Clouseau in the *Pink Panther* films **34** *The Lavender Hill Mob* **35** Peter Cushing **36** *A Hard Day's Night* **37** Ben Kingsley **38** Ken Loach **39** *A Streetcar Named Desire* (1951) **40** Simone Signoret **41** Peter O'Toole **42** Michael Caine **43** 1954 **44** Helen Mirren **45** Alan Bennett **46** *The Remains of the Day* **47** Daphne du Maurier **48** Richard Griffiths **49** George Formby **50** *The Italian Job*

FLORA AND FAUNA QUIZ ANSWERS FROM PAGE 50

1 Ink **2** Poseidon **3** Berkshire. The Ankerwycke Yew tree is found close to the ruins of the 12th-century St Mary's Priory near Wraysbury **4** Orford Ness in Suffolk **5** The otter **6** Parapoxvirus disease. Since the introduction of the grey squirrel in the 1870s, the red squirrel population has declined from around 3.5 million to up to 160,000 individuals **7** Pine martens **8** Elder **9** Beatrix Potter **10** Six – common European adder (*Vipera berus*), grass snake (*Natrix natrix*), smooth snake (*Coronella austriaca*), common lizard (*Lacerta vivipara*), sand lizard (*Lacerta agilis*) and slow worm (*Anguis fragilis*) **11** Sylvia Plath in *The Collected Poems* **12** Thomas Hardy **13** The glow-worm (*Lampyris noctiluca*), which is actually a beetle **14** The hop, which is used in brewing **15** Sir Edwin Landseer's portrait of a red deer stag was commissioned for the Palace of Westminster **16** St Cuthbert, who lived on Inner Farne for eight years in the 7th-century and gave sanctuary to eider ducks ("Cuddy's") in stormy weather **17** Dandelion **18** Devil's-bit scabious **19** The Sussex Emerald moth **20** Pike **21** Bladderwrack – a common seaweed **22** The Wash on the east coast of England where the counties of Norfolk and Lincolnshire meet **23** Charles Rothschild, who in May 1912 held a meeting at the Natural History Museum in London to form the Society for the Promotion of Nature Reserves, which today is called The Wildlife Trusts **24** Dragonfly, one of the most common in Europe **25** Marram grass **26** Collared dove **27** Major Oak in Sherwood Forest in Nottinghamshire **28** West Bromwich Albion FC **29** 1964 **30** *The Badger* by John Clare

LANDMARKS OF ENGLAND CROSSWORD ANSWERS FROM PAGE 79

ACROSS: **8** Kent **9** Gateshead **10** Brontë **11** Earl Grey **12** Carlyle **14** Bygones **17** Skiff **18** Cathedral **21** Isis **23** Mural **24** Wash **25** Guardsman **27** Banks **30** Cheddar **32** Pudding **34** November **36** Forest **38** St Austell **39** Iron

DOWN: **1** Deer park **2** Eton **3** HG Wells **4** Steel **5** Osprey **6** Wedgwood **7** Edge **13** Lifts **15** Evans **16** Hadrian **19** Helm **20** Imps **22** South **24** Weald **26** Ridgeway **28** Kingston **29** Suffolk **31** Abbess **33** Arden **35** Oast **37** Ruin

A BRIEF HISTORY OF THIS ENGLAND

AS of spring 2021, it has been 53 years since *This England* magazine first appeared on the news stand. Roy Faiers was, of course, the editor and set out his vision for his new magazine.

"I hope you find enjoyment among its pages, for we shall seek to capture the true spirit of England in every edition. We shall not be slick or sensational. There will be no world scoop articles, no glamour pictures, no fierce controversies. Instead, we have set out deliberately to produce a wholesome, straightforward and gentle magazine that loves its own dear land and the people who have sprung from its soil.

"Instead of politics we shall bring you the poetry of the English countryside in words and pictures. Instead of bigotry we shall portray the beauty of our towns and villages. Instead of prejudice there will be pride in our ancient traditions, the surviving crafts, the legends, the life, the splendour and peace of this England."

The magazine was popular from the start, with readers enjoying its unique and gentle celebration of their country. In its 53 years, it has covered everything from surnames of famous football managers to the lace villages of England, from Daphne du Maurier's Cornwall to World War I cigarette cards.

The first cover and covers through the years

As befits a magazine whose slogan is "as refreshing as a pot of tea", we've celebrated England's finest tea rooms, and we've visited churches the length and breadth of the country. We've explored towns, cities and villages. Our diverse and talented contributors have told the stories of forgotten heroes and under-appreciated eccentrics.

Our Royal History must be one of the longest-running magazine series ever, at a whopping 50 parts so far! Our other regulars include Historic Homes of England, Great Britons, Gardener's Notes, Explore England and our regular round-up of obscure stories and goings-on in Cornucopia. Although sometimes the magazine takes a nostalgic look at things, we find plenty to celebrate in modern England.

The annual gives a flavour of the unique mix that is *This England.* Our events pages at the start of each of our sections cover some of our most unique traditions and customs of the year from the high profile such as Ascot, Henley and Wimbledon to our more eccentric pastimes – the wife-carrying championships in Dorking spring to mind, or the World's Biggest Liar competition in Santon Bridge.

Along with these, we have quizzes galore to test your knowledge of geography, landmarks, wildlife and classic films. We celebrate the anniversary of the zany *Goon Show*, the 75th anniversary of school milk and 125 years since Blackpool Pleasure Beach was founded. Fiona Stapley visits her favourite British pubs, plus our best-known birds are profiled (with a poem about each one), and Simon Sebag Montefiore writes about this country's greatest orators. There's plenty more to dip into, too.

If you've enjoyed the annual, our subscription offer overleaf is great value, either for yourself or for an Anglophile friend.